Key Stage 3
Developing Literacy

TEXT LEVEL

READING AND WRITING ACTIVITIES
FOR LITERACY LESSONS

year

7

Christine Moorcroft and Ray Barker

A & C BLACK

Contents

Speaking and listening

Glossary

Acknowledgements
The authors and publishers are grateful for permission to reproduce the following:
p. 12 extract from *The Usborne Book of Science* by Amanda Kent and Alan Ward, reproduced by permission of Usborne Publishing. Copyright © 1987 Usborne Publishing Ltd; **p. 14** extract from *Letts Study Guide: Key Stage 3 History* by Peter Lane and Christopher Lane (Letts, 1999); **p. 16** extract from *Buddha: A Beginner's Guide* by Gillian Stokes (Hodder & Stoughton, 2000). Reproduced by permission of Hodder Arnold; **p. 18** extract from www.foodstandards.gov.uk/healthiereating/dailydiet/ (Crown copyright); **p. 20** extract from *Holes* by Louis Sachar (Bloomsbury Children's Books, 2000); **p. 22** 'Cool Medium' by David Sutton from *Absences and Celebrations* (Chatto & Windus, 1982). Reprinted by permission of The Random House Group Ltd; **p. 24** extract from *19 Magazine*, February 2002 (IPC Magazines); **p. 25** extract from *Period Ideas*, February 2003 (Aceville Publications); **p. 26** extract from *I Am David* by Anne Holm. English translation © 1965. First published 1963 as *David* by Gyldendal, Copenhagen. Used with the permission of Egmont Books Limited; **p. 28** 'Tarantella' from *Sonnets and Verse* by Hilaire Belloc (Gerald Duckworth & Co, 1954). Reprinted by permission of PFD on behalf of The Estate of Hilaire Belloc © 1970, The Estate of Hilaire Belloc; **p. 32** 'Art Year Haikus' by John Kitching from *The Works: Every Kind of Poem You Will Ever Need for the Literacy Hour*, edited by Paul Cookson (Macmillan Children's Books, 2000); **p. 36** extract from 'The Star Beast' from *Mainly in Moonlight* by Nicholas Stuart Grey (Faber and Faber, 1965); **p. 42** 'The Shape of a Poem' by Chris Ogden from *What Shape is a Poem?* edited by Paul Cookson (Macmillan Children's Books, 2002); **p. 43** 'Electric Guitars' from *Cars Stars Electric Guitars* by James Carter © 2002 James Carter. Reprinted by permission of Walker Books Ltd; **p. 44** extract from *Greek and Roman Life* by Ian Jenkins (British Museum Press, 1986); **p. 50** extract from *As I Walked Out One Midsummer Morning* by Laurie Lee (Andre Deutsch, 1969); **p. 51** extract from *The Mouse and His Child* by Russell Hoban (Faber Children's Books, 1969); **p. 52** extract from *Animal Farm* by George Orwell (Copyright © George Orwell, 1945) by permission of Bill Hamilton as the Literary Executor of The Estate of the Late Sonia Brownell Orwell and Secker & Warburg Ltd; **pp. 62–63** extracts from *The Owl Service* by Alan Garner (Collins, 1995). Reprinted by permission of HarperCollins Publishers Ltd © Alan Garner, 1995.

Published 2004 by A & C Black Publishers Limited
37 Soho Square, London W1D 3QZ
www.acblack.com

ISBN 0-7136-6486-X

Copyright text © Christine Moorcroft and Ray Barker, 2004
Copyright illustrations © David Benham, 2004
Copyright cover illustration © Paul Cemmick, 2004
Editor: Lucy Poddington

The authors and publishers would like to thank Claire Truman for her advice in producing this series of books.

A CIP catalogue record for this book is available from the British Library.

Printed in Great Britain by St Edmundsbury Press Ltd, Bury St Edmunds, Suffolk.

A & C Black uses paper produced with elemental chlorine-free pulp, harvested from managed sustainable forests.

Introduction

Key Stage 3 Developing Literacy: Text Level is a series of photocopiable resources for Years 7, 8 and 9, designed to be used during English lessons or in other subjects across the curriculum to improve reading, writing, and speaking and listening skills. The activities are also ideal for homework. The books focus on the Text level strand of the Key Stage 3 National Strategy *Framework for teaching English: Years 7, 8 and 9*.

Each book supports the teaching of English by providing a series of activities that develop essential literacy skills. These include reading and the interpretation of texts (fiction and non-fiction), writing and the communication of ideas for specific purposes and in appropriate styles – as well as speaking and listening. All of these are about communication, and demand that the reader, writer or speaker is in control of his or her material and uses language appropriately.

Text Level Year 7 develops the pupils' appreciation and awareness of each of these aspects. In particular, it helps them to understand the need to tailor a text to match the needs of specific audiences and purposes. The pupils are encouraged to develop skills in a way that is progressive as well as transferable to different contexts. These skills include:

- reading to extract information and deduce meaning;
- investigating how writers enhance meaning and convey setting, character and mood;
- structuring a story and portraying character;
- organising texts in ways appropriate to their content;
- expressing a personal view, orally and in writing;
- interacting effectively in group discussion.

How to use this book

Each double-page spread in this book is based on a Year 7 Text level objective. The left-hand page is a **starter** activity, which may be an OHT for use with the whole class, or an activity for the pupils to work on in pairs or small groups. The right-hand page provides a **consolidation** activity to reinforce the main teaching objective, followed by an **extension** activity (**Now try this!**) to extend the pupils' learning.

Starter activities

Each starter activity is designed to be used as a short introduction to the consolidation activity that follows it. Evidence has shown that lessons which start with a sharp focus on a specific objective – for only ten to fifteen minutes – grab the pupils' attention and ensure that the whole class is clear about what to do and about the expected outcome of the lesson. The starter activities in this book address the objectives in a direct and explicit way. They involve both reading and writing, and encourage fast-paced learning and interaction. Various teaching and learning styles are used – from independent to teacher supported – focusing on the following key teacher interactions:

- direction
- modelling
- explanation
- exploration
- discussion
- demonstration
- scaffolding
- questioning
- investigation
- reflection and evaluation.

The starter activities in this book also provide valuable opportunities to revise previous learning. New terms are introduced and other important terms are revised during the starter activity; these are highlighted by being boxed or set in bold type. All the highlighted terms are explained in the glossary on page 64, which can be photocopied for the pupils to file and use for reference.

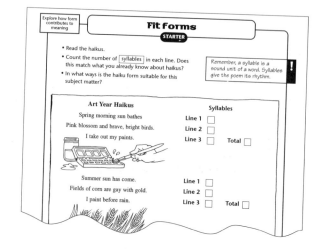

The starter activities can be photocopied and used in the following ways:

- as an OHT for whole-class teaching, with pupils giving answers orally or coming to the front to help complete the sheet;
- as a group activity, with each group working through the sheet or with different groups focusing on different parts of the sheet;
- as a timed activity, with the pupils completing as much of the sheet as possible within a time limit;
- in conjunction with appropriate class texts to help illustrate a principle;
- as preparatory work for an investigation, to be carried out for homework;
- as a stand-alone revision sheet for groups or individuals;
- as a tool for assessment.

Consolidation activities

The *Framework for teaching English: Years 7, 8 and 9* advocates that lessons should continue with a development of the main teaching points. The consolidation activities in this book can be used as the focus of this development, freeing teachers to work intensively with groups or individuals on the current objective.

The instructions in the activities are presented clearly to enable pupils to work independently. There are also opportunities for the pupils to work in pairs or groups, to encourage discussion and co-operation. Hints and reminders are given in boxes at the page margin.

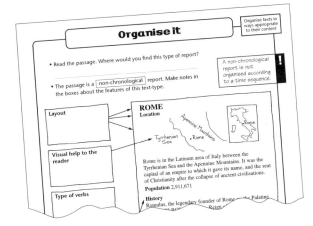

Extension activities

Each page ends with a **Now try this!** extension activity. These more challenging activities may be appropriate for only some of the pupils; it is not expected that the whole class should complete them. The pupils may need to record their answers in a notebook or on a separate piece of paper.

Organisation

The activities require very few resources besides dictionaries and thesauruses. Occasionally it may be useful to have available examples of texts such as: fictional and non-fictional recounts, reports (from booklets, leaflets and reference books), discussions and arguments (from newspapers, magazines or the Internet), and persuasive texts such as advertisements and charity or political leaflets. For some of the activities the pupils will need access to the Internet and resources in the school library.

All the activities in this book are linked closely to the requirements of the *Framework for teaching English*, but it is not intended that they should be presented in any specific order, unless stated. This resource is versatile and is intended for teachers to use according to the literacy needs of their pupils.

Some of the activities can be linked with work in other subjects; however, it is envisaged that most of the activities will be carried out during English lessons.

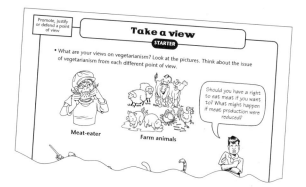

Teachers' notes

The notes provided at the foot of the activity pages contain additional instructions for using the sheets. These can be masked before photocopying. The notes on pages 6–9 offer further practical advice on making the most of the activity sheets, including extra lesson ideas and suggestions for introducing the teaching objectives.

Useful websites

Websites which you may find useful include: www.gutenberg.net, www.bartleby.com and www.penguinclassics.com (for access to a range of free texts), www.shakespeares-globe.org and www.shakespeare.com (for Shakespeare resources), www.englishresources.co.uk (for English resources, including units of work), www.literatureproject.com/ (a collection of classic books, poems, speeches and plays) and http://vtc.ngfl.gov.uk/docserver.php (Virtual Teacher Centre – a wealth of resources and information on literacy and other subjects).

Teachers' notes

The notes below expand upon those provided at the foot of each activity page. They give ideas for making the most of the activity sheets, including suggestions for follow-up work and answers to selected activities.

Reading

Quick skim (pages 10–11). This activity develops the pupils' skills in skimming a text to work out whether it will help them find the information they need. The **starter** activity gives an example of how to evaluate books before deciding which to buy, or borrow from a library. In the **consolidation** activity and **extension** activity (**Now try this!**), the pupils select and skim books to help them answer a question. Staff from another department could suggest suitable questions for them to research. The pupils are encouraged to look at clues such as chapter headings and the index, rather than reading the book from cover to cover. The activity also prepares for selective note-making.

Index search (pages 12–13). This activity helps the pupils to understand and use the index of a book. The **starter** activity focuses on the purpose of an index and how a writer compiles it. The index should help readers to find quickly the relevant sections of the book for the information they are looking for. In this passage, words and phrases which should be indexed include *absorb/absorption, atom, bond, carbon dioxide, chemical reaction, chlorine, compound, element, energy, gas, heat, mixture, salt, separate/separation, sodium, sodium chloride*. The **consolidation** activity helps the pupils to develop skills in using an index to find information quickly. The answers are: (1) true, (2) false, (3) false, (4) true, (5) true, (6) false, (7) true, (8) true, (9) false, (10) true, (11) true, (12) false. The word in the grid is *SPIT*.

Key words (pages 14–15). Key words are vital for carrying out an effective Internet search; the more accurately key words are used, the fewer irrelevant websites will be listed. Using an index also involves deciding which are the key words in a topic. The **starter** activity helps the pupils to identify the key words in a history text by looking for the answers to questions. This is a quick way of appraising the usefulness of a text as well as finding relevant information. The answers to questions 2, 3 and 4 can be found in the passage. The **consolidation** and **extension** activities involve listing key words and phrases on a range of topics and using them for research.

Make a note (pages 16–17). Many pupils have difficulty in deciding how much to write when they take notes. This activity helps them to take notes and write 'in their own words'. The **starter** activity prepares for note-taking by encouraging them to read a passage quickly and to identify useful words and phrases. The **consolidation** activity provides a framework which helps them to make notes from the passage. In the **extension** activity the pupils use their notes to write a paragraph in their own words, building up sentences from their notes. They can assess whether they have successfully used their own words by comparing what they have written with the passage in the starter activity.

Web versus books (pages 18–19). This activity asks the pupils to use books and the Internet to look for similar types of information. In the **starter** activity they analyse how they use the Internet for research. The **consolidation** activity encourages the pupils to compare ways in which they use books and the Internet. They can use the website provided or www.bbc.co.uk/health/nutrition/. They should appreciate the advantages and disadvantages of each medium: for example, when using a website it is usually easy to move from page to page and to return to the starting point using the Back button, whereas in a book it is less easy to follow a route without using many stickers and bookmarks. An advantage of books is having information at hand without having to find a computer, but where large books such as encyclopedias are concerned this is not an advantage, since they are too big to carry around. Websites, like books, become out of date, but they can be updated more quickly and easily than printed text.

Be an active reader (pages 20–21). This encourages the pupils to think about fiction they read, to ensure that they understand it and to recognise the ways in which it affects them. In the **starter** activity, the writer of the passage reveals facts about Stanley in an expressionless and emotionless way and, in doing so, paints a picture of a boy whose emotions are numbed by his experiences. This numbness is heightened by comparison (the snapshot memories of pleasant experiences of his childhood compared with painful experiences). The details build up a picture of Stanley's life and the ways in which he responds to other people. The **consolidation** and **extension** activities encourage the pupils to analyse other passages in a similar way, using evidence from the text to support their responses.

What does it say? (pages 22–23). This activity encourages the pupils to look for meaning in what they read. The message of the poem in the **starter** activity is that television stopped children playing outdoors (*Got television and disappeared indoors... instead of coming out*); not only that, it is as if it robbed them of life (*moon-grey flickers / From a dead planet... Is life / Something to be given up for that?*); and people who do not conform are considered odd (*Amused, superior, grown-up faces smile: / The awkward child...*). The **consolidation** activity continues the investigation of the messages in the poem by looking at contrasts: life (*clamour of wild games*) and death (*silent woods, moon-grey flickers, dead planet, curtained windows*); natural (*hedgerow, first-starred, batwinged dusks of autumn, woodland, trees and winter stars*) and unnatural (*moon-grey flickers, strange communion*); modern (*television*) and old-fashioned (*to toast crusts over stick fires, antique*); sensible, sophisticated, 'normal' (*amused, superior, grown-up faces smile*) and silly, naïve, not 'normal' (*sulked, refused their invitations, awkward child, stalks, heresy*). A note of hope is suggested in the line *As if one day the others might come back.*

Who is the audience? (pages 24–25). This activity looks at passages from two contrasting magazines, aimed at very different audiences. The **starter** activity gives the pupils hints to help them decide how formal a text is. The passage is from *19* Magazine, a fashion magazine aimed at 19-year-olds but probably read by younger people. The informal, lively style suggests a sense of fun through the use of exclamations. The tone is friendly, appealing directly to the reader. Contractions and slang expressions (such as *wicked* and *Yikes!*) are used. The passage in the **consolidation** activity is from *Period Ideas* magazine and therefore appeals to older readers. The register is more formal, although the occasional contraction is used along with common idioms such as *dim and distant* and *finishing touches*. As a follow-up, the pupils could rewrite each passage in a way that would make the subject matter appeal to a different audience. They should give reasons for the changes they make.

Character and mood (pages 26–27). This activity focuses on the ways in which writers create a setting and develop a character. In the passage in the **starter** activity, David has escaped from a concentration camp. He has arrived in Italy having stowed away on a ship. The narrative of David's thoughts and actions develops the character and setting and evokes the reader's sympathy for him. The writer uses dialogue overheard by David to give information about what David looks like. In the **consolidation** activity, the pupils investigate specific ways in which character and mood are conveyed in the passage. The **extension** activity asks them to apply what they have learned to a passage by a different writer.

Lively language (pages 28–29). This activity looks at the effect of language choices. In the **starter** activity, the poem's lively rhythm and evocative language conjure up an image of people taking part in a boisterous dance to the sound of clapping, guitar music and the stamping of feet. At the beginning and end of the poem, there are contrasting quiet, wistful parts. Even though the lines are of the same length as some of those in the lively section of the poem, the words themselves create a slower movement, for example:

Lively	Wistful
Glancing,	Never more;
Dancing,	Miranda,
Backing and advancing,	Never more.

The **consolidation** activity focuses on the effects of internal rhyme in the poem. The pupils are asked to replace certain words with synonyms, and to notice how this changes the rhythm.

A reading journal (pages 30–31). This activity encourages the pupils to think in a critical and reflective way about books they read. The **starter** activity provides a model of how to identify the good points and any weaknesses of a book. It also demonstrates how to expand answers: for example, the book is essentially about word derivations, but the writer of the journal elaborates on the way in which it deals with words and the kinds of words it covers. In the **consolidation** activity the pupils are encouraged to consider their own responses to a book: whether they like it and what they like about it; how they react to it (and, possibly, how other people react to it). They should remember that any sensible response is acceptable as long as it is supported by evidence.

Fit forms (pages 32–33). This focuses on the haiku form, which originated in Japan for writing poems about nature. The **starter** activity looks at the syllable pattern of the three lines (5, 7, 5) which naturally creates a smooth, calm rhythm, suitable for serene nature poems. The final line usually adds a twist or a new thought to the haiku. In the **consolidation** activity the pupils write haikus of their own. It is difficult to write a haiku that has a fast pace and a mood of excitement or urgency; as a follow-up, the pupils could try writing a haiku about a dramatic natural event (such as a storm or an earthquake) to explore the difficulties.

Writing

A perfect plan (pages 34–35). This activity revises the idea of planning a passage using paragraphs and then moves on to other ways of collecting and assembling ideas. The **starter** activity uses a passage linked to a history topic to show how the writer sets the scene, develops the idea, provides information and then concludes. The **consolidation** activity gives the pupils two formats for planning: a sequential list (flow chart) and a star chart, where the ideas develop from the topic in the centre. These two different formats will be useful for different kinds of writing. Instructions would be better in a flow chart whereas a report or a discussion may work better with ideas coming from a central point.

Structure it (pages 36–37). The importance of story structure is reinforced in this activity. The **starter** activity uses a passage from the opening of a science fiction story which makes the reader want to read on by describing the arrival at a farm of a mysterious creature. The **consolidation** activity encourages the pupils to structure a story so that it has a clear beginning, middle and end. It invites them to introduce a complication in the story which leads to a crisis. This can then be used to drive forward the story until it reaches a satisfactory conclusion.

Create a character (pages 38–39). This activity focuses on how a writer can portray character through describing what the character looks like and what he or she says and does. The **starter** activity uses two character descriptions by Charles Dickens. The choice of adjectives shows that Mrs Gamp – although a drunk – is not an unlikeable character; she is merely an eccentric. Miss Murdstone, on the other hand, is portrayed as a harsh, unfeeling character. The **consolidation** activity provides a writing format to enable the pupils to plan and structure their writing. The **extension** activity highlights the difference between purely factual descriptions (for example, police descriptions) and those used in fiction.

Said and done (pages 40–41). Here, work on portraying character is developed by looking closely at what a character's actions and words reveal. The passage in the **starter** activity portrays the ambiguous character of Long John Silver. He is mysterious and vaguely threatening, yet others respect him and he is always pleasant to Jim Hawkins, the narrator of the novel. The **consolidation** activity provides a writing format to help the pupils write a passage about a familiar fictional character. The **extension** activity asks them to change the hero into a villain (or vice versa), by adapting the language, dialogue and the character's actions. As a follow-up, the pupils could investigate and compare the ways characters are portrayed in other texts they are studying.

Shape and sound (pages 42–43). This activity encourages the pupils to experiment with the sound and the look of words to achieve particular effects. The **starter** activity presents a shape poem in which the words of the poem make the shapes described. The **consolidation** activity continues with the theme and invites the pupils to look at how alliteration and onomatopoeia contribute to the effect of a shape poem. The **extension** activity gives the pupils the opportunity to create their own shape poem. A snake is an ideal subject, since the words chosen can be full of hissing s sounds (the word *hissing* itself is onomatopoeic) and the words of the poem can 'snake' across the page.

Organise it (pages 44–45). This activity looks at ways in which information texts can be organised. In the **starter** activity the pupils investigate a report from a history book. Reports systematically organise and record factual information. The structure depends upon the aim of the report; here each paragraph deals with a different aspect of Roman dress. Reports may contain technical vocabulary, denoted by the use of italics. The **consolidation** activity looks at a non-chronological report from a travel guidebook. It is organised through the use of sub-headings to categorise the information. Other layout features include bold headings, capitals for the main heading and the use of diagrams – all of which help the reader to understand and follow the text easily.

Make it clear (pages 46–47). This activity encourages the pupils to give and evaluate instructions and directions. The passage in the **starter** activity shows the characteristic features of instructions: imperative verbs; direct language (sometimes using *you*); the present tense; mainly the active voice; short, simple sentences; and the use of numbered points and diagrams. In the **consolidation** activity the pupils are asked to give directions using a map. They will need to use precise language so that the audience can understand its exact meaning. The **extension** activity is a speaking and listening task in which the pupils evaluate directions given by a partner.

Describe in detail (pages 48–49). This activity reinforces that a description must be suited to the purpose of the writing and the audience for whom it is written. In the **starter** activity the pupils are asked to write scientific descriptions using labelled diagrams as a starting point. The **consolidation** activity focuses on imaginative description, which has a very different purpose and audience. The activity helps the pupils to write imaginatively about autumn leaves using appropriate adjectives and figurative language. The **extension** activity provides further practice in writing scientific and fictional descriptions and reinforces the pupils' understanding of the differences between the two types. As a follow-up, the pupils could investigate the use of descriptive language in other texts they are studying.

People and places (pages 50–51). This activity looks at how writers use language to build up an impression of people and places. The passage in the **starter** activity is an evocative description of a place, with some words missing. The pupils are asked to choose words which best suit the description. The missing words are: (A) *smoother*, (B) *rust-corroded*, (C) *rotting*, (D) *flooded*, (E) *broken glass*, (F) *blue*, (G) *streams*, (H) *drag*, (I) *shreds*, (J) *smouldering*, (K) *flare*. Although the words the author used are 'correct', the pupils may give alternatives if they can provide adequate reasons for their choices. The **consolidation** activity features a description of a character which uses detail in a similar way to build up an impression. From the start of the passage, suspicion is aroused by the *large rat* and the way he *crept out of the shadows*. Language such as *greasy*, *dirty*, *stale* and *beadily* confirm that the rat is the villain of the story. The **extension** activity gives the pupils an opportunity to write their own description of a villain using similar techniques.

Persuasive power (pages 52–53). In this activity the pupils investigate persuasive language. The **starter** activity looks at a passage from *Animal Farm* in which Major speaks to the animals and persuades them to revolt. He does this through involving his audience by addressing them directly, giving evidence to support his case and using rhetorical devices (rhetorical questions and repetition of key phrases). The **consolidation** and **extension** activities help the pupils to form a personal view on the issue of corporal punishment in schools, and to write a persuasive speech using the features they have learned about.

Rave reviews (pages 54–55). The lively reviews in the **starter** activity are aimed at teenagers; this is reflected in the language and ideas. The book review has a clear structure: it introduces the subject matter, then explains why young people should find the book useful; it suggests a problem in the language, and ends with a positive recommendation. The video and DVD review gives an introduction to the product, refers to general features which might appeal, mentions a weakness in the product and ends with a recommendation and a caution that it may not be suitable for all viewers. The **consolidation** activity provides writing formats to help the pupils write reviews of their own.

Speaking and listening

Take a view (pages 56–57). This activity helps to develop the pupils' speaking and listening skills and build their confidence in this area. The **starter** activity involves preparing for an oral task in which they justify and defend a view on the issue of vegetarianism. The **consolidation** activity asks the pupils to choose a statement and prepare a speech to support or oppose it. The activity encourages them to consider how persuasive language will improve their speech and provides some examples of useful phrases. They could also refer to the words and phrases in the extension activity on page 53.

The way it's said (pages 58–59). This activity focuses on the ways in which people naturally change the way they speak in different situations. The **starter** activity gives examples of how speakers match the level of formality of their language to the situation. In the **consolidation** activity, the pupils listen to formal and informal interviews and notice the differences in the ways people speak. They may need help in distinguishing between accent and dialect, dialect and slang, and standard and non-standard English. They should be aware that non-standard English is not inferior to standard English and each has its place, depending on the audience, purpose and context.

Save me! (pages 60–61). This activity uses a 'balloon debate' as a way of speaking in role for a purpose. The **starter** activity introduces the balloon debate format by asking the pupils, in groups, to agree on a character to be saved. The **consolidation** activity provides a structure to help the pupils research a person (who could be real or fictional, living or from history) and plan a speech in role to persuade an audience why they should be saved.

Speech detectives (pages 62–63). This activity encourages the pupils to experiment with language in different roles. The **starter** activity encourages them to notice how the type of language used in spoken words tells us about the speakers and the situation. In the **consolidation** activity they use what they have learned to adapt a dialogue to a different situation. The pupils could read out their dialogues in role to prompt a discussion of how tone of voice, actions and body language add to the spoken words.

Quick skim
STARTER

Jenna's Border Collie, Bracken, is at his happiest when he is chasing bikes. The cyclists do not share his happiness. Jenna is looking for a book to help her train Bracken to come to her whenever she calls him.

- Read what Jenna says to herself about each book she looks at. Decide which one will be the most helpful.
- Explain your choice.

1 *Training Your Dog* has a chapter called 'Training', with the sub-headings 'Sit', 'Stay', 'Rewards', 'House-training'. The index lists 'down', 'rewards', 'sit' and 'stay'.

2 This one is called *Understanding the Border Collie*. There's a chapter on 'The Growing Collie'. It has sub-headings 'The Art of Control', 'Training, Disobedience and the Collie Mind' and 'Recall'. Another chapter called 'Common Collie Behavioural Problems' has sub-headings 'Chasing', 'Nipping' and 'Over-boisterousness'. The index lists 'chasing', 'commands' and a whole section on 'obedience'.

3 *Your New Puppy* has no index. Chapter headings are 'Choosing a Puppy', 'Feeding', 'Training' and 'Health and Hygiene'. There might be something in 'Training' – bullet points begin with the words 'sit', 'stay', 'leave' and 'down'.

4 Here's one called *Border Collies*. It contains lots of photographs of different Border Collies. It has chapters on the history of the breed, working dogs (with sub-headings about the different work they can be trained for), rescue dogs and breeders. The index lists breeders and trainers.

5 *The Story of Meg.* This is the life story of a Border Collie from a rescue centre. It is written in chronological order, as a diary (but not with every single day filled in). On some days there are recounts of how Meg's owner taught her to be obedient.

6 *How to Train Your Dog* has a back cover blurb which says 'What do you want your dog to do? What don't you want it to do? This is the book you've been waiting for.' There is no index. The contents page lists things people want their dogs to do: 'Sit', 'Stay', 'Down', 'Leave', 'Heel', then it lists things people don't want their dogs to do: 'Biting', 'Chewing furniture', 'Chasing bikes and cars'. Each chapter has a drawing of a dog doing one of these things, with a short block of text alongside.

Teachers' note Photocopy this page onto an OHT. Read the speech bubbles with the pupils and encourage them to suggest which book they think would be the most helpful to Jenna. Then ask them what might be useful in the book, and how they can tell that the book will help. Discuss how well Jenna goes about evaluating each book. Explain that being able to 'skim' books to gain an overview of the subject matter will save the pupils time, as it is much quicker than reading a book from cover to cover (and possibly finding it unhelpful).

10

Developing Literacy
Text Level
Year 7
© A & C BLACK

Quick skim

- Write a question to which you want to find the answer. _____

- Find books you think might be useful. List them on the chart.

- Skim the books. Make a note on the chart of useful chapters, index entries and page numbers.

Title, author, publisher and date	Useful chapters	Useful index entries and the pages to look at

- List any other ways in which you can tell whether a resource is going to be useful.

- Choose two other resources and use your ideas to evaluate how useful they will be for answering your question. Discuss this with a partner.

- Skim the resources and make notes on a chart like the one above.

Teachers' note Before the lesson, ask the pupils to formulate a question which they need to answer for work in another subject. They could work in pairs. They will need access to books on the chosen topic. For the extension activity, you could provide extra copies of the chart.

Developing Literacy
Text Level
Year 7
© A & C BLACK

Index search
STARTER

- Read the passage.
- Underline the words you think should be in the book's index.
- Explain your choices.

How will the index help readers? Think about what readers might want to find out from the book.

!

What is a chemical reaction?
A chemical reaction, or change, occurs when new substances form. This happens when the bonds between atoms or groups of atoms are broken and rearranged to form new compounds. The bonds between them are often strong and this explains why energy, usually in the form of heat, is needed to start a reaction.

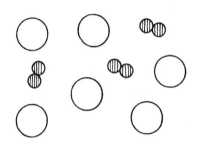

Before the reaction

What makes a chemical reaction take place?
When a chemical reaction takes place, heat is usually absorbed or given out. Unlike mixtures, compounds have different properties from those of the elements they contain. For example, sodium and chlorine are both dangerous. But they combine with each other to form sodium chloride, which is the salt you eat.

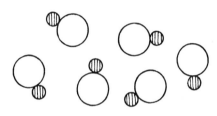

After the reaction

Baking a cake
If you mix together butter, sugar, flour and baking powder, you get a mixture which still looks, tastes and feels like its ingredients. But when liquid is added and it is cooked, you can see that a chemical reaction has taken place. The baking powder reacts with the other ingredients to give off bubbles of gas (carbon dioxide), which makes the mixture rise. The new substance looks, feels and tastes different from the uncooked mixture and cannot be separated back into the original ingredients. When you make a cake, it is important to get the quantities right, or the cake may not rise. It is just the same in other chemical reactions.

From *The Usborne Book of Science* by Amanda Kent and Alan Ward

These bubbles are made by carbon dioxide gas.

Teachers' note Photocopy this page onto an OHT. First ensure that the pupils know the differences in appearance and purpose between an index and a glossary. Discuss how readers use an index, and ask the pupils what kind of words they would find helpful in an index. Read the passage with the pupils and invite several of them to come and underline the words in the text which they think should be in the index. They should explain their choices. Encourage the rest of the class to comment on the choices and to suggest any other words they think should be included.

Developing Literacy
Text Level
Year 7
© A & C BLACK

Index search

- Read the statements on the chart. Choose an information book that will help you to find out whether the statements are true or false.

- From which subject do the statements come? _____

- What topic are they about? _____

- What is the title of the book you have chosen? _____

_____

- Use the index of your book to find the information. Tick true or false.
- If the statement is true, colour its number in the grid.

Statement	True	False	Colour number:
A headland is an area of hard rock that juts out into the sea.			1
A stack is a rock formation beneath the surface of the sea.			2
A stack is formed by volcanic action.			3
Coastal erosion is caused by the action of the sea.			4
Corrasion or abrasion is erosion in which waves pick up material such as pieces of stone and hurl it at the base of a cliff, wearing away the rock.			5
Hydraulic action is erosion caused when waves break up rocks and pebbles by making them bump into one another.			6
Corrosion or solution is when cliffs are eroded by weak acids in the sea.			7
Erosion at the base of a cliff causes cliff recession.			8
Destructive waves build beaches.			9
A destructive wave is high in proportion to its length.			10
A destructive wave has a strong backwash.			11
The fetch of a wave is its height.			12

2	6	9	3	12	3	3	2	6	9	2	12	9	9	2
6	1	4	8	2	7	7	5	3	11	3	10	1	4	3
12	10	2	9	6	8	3	4	3	10	9	11	5	7	9
3	4	7	8	3	10	1	11	12	4	9	2	8	3	6
12	6	6	10	12	5	6	9	2	5	2	6	5	3	6
9	3	9	11	2	7	3	2	3	7	3	12	10	2	9
2	1	5	7	9	5	12	6	12	1	6	3	8	9	12

You will reveal the name of a geographical feature.

NOW TRY THIS!

- For each incorrect statement, write a correct version.

Use the book's glossary or a dictionary to help. !

Teachers' note The pupils will need access to information books that will help them to find out about the statements on the chart. They could work in pairs. During the plenary session, discuss how the pupils used the index, and any problems they had in locating the information.

Developing Literacy
Text Level
Year 7
© A & C BLACK

Key words

STARTER

• Read the passage.

William I

Some of Harold's followers were angry at William's success and others refused to accept Norman rule. William had to cope with many rebellions. So how did he manage to impose Norman rule on England?

① He promised to follow 'saintly Edward's' laws and customs.

② He acted as owner of all the land. He kept a quarter for himself, gave the Church a quarter, and rewarded Normans with most of the rest.

③ He and his Norman barons built castles from which they imposed their rule on the surrounding areas.

④ Although his barons had sworn an oath of loyalty to him, William knew that, in Edward's England and his own Normandy, powerful landowners had challenged their overlord's power. They relied on the support of the knights to whom they had sub-let some of their land, and from whom they got an oath of loyalty. So in 1086, William made every landowner swear an oath of loyalty to him personally.

⑤ William spent Christmas 1085 at his Gloucester estate: he and other landowners went from one estate to another to 'live off the produce of their land'. It was at Gloucester that William decided to find out exactly what went on in his kingdom. His shire officers worked so efficiently that by the time he came to Salisbury in August 1086 they could give him the pages of sheepskin, sewn together to form a book, which contained all the details he had asked for. The book was so complete that it was soon called the Domesday Book because people compared it with what might happen on the Last Day of Judgement.

From *Letts Study Guide: Key Stage 3 History* by Peter Lane and Christopher Lane

• From which subject does the passage come? _____

• What topic is it about? _____

• Which of these questions does the passage help you to answer? Tick or cross the boxes.

• For each question you tick, underline the key words and phrases in the passage. Use a different colour for each question.

1. How did William become king of England? ☐

2. How did William rule his kingdom? ☐

3. Who were the most powerful people in England in William's reign? ☐

4. How did William find out about the kingdom he was ruling? ☐

5. How did William deal with invasions of his kingdom? ☐

Teachers' note Photocopy this page onto an OHT. You could begin by reading the passage with the pupils and asking them what each numbered section is about. They could suggest sub-headings for each section which summarise the contents. Invite the pupils to contribute to the completion of the OHT. Explain that key words and phrases indicate the topic of a passage or paragraph. It will be helpful to colour-code questions 1 to 5 and to underline the key words in the passage using the appropriate colours.

Developing Literacy
Text Level
Year 7
© A & C BLACK

Key words

You can use **key words and phrases** to help you search for information on the Internet or on CD-ROMs.

- Think of key words or phrases which could help you to find out about these topics.

List at least three for each topic. !

Topic	Key words or phrases
(a) industries in Japan	*economy,*
(b) the effects of the sea on coastlines	
(c) river formations	
(d) inland flooding in Britain	
(e) immigration in Britain	
(f) the effects of an earthquake	
(g) how volcanoes occur	

- Choose one of the topics. Use your key words or phrases to search for information on the Internet or on CD-ROMs.
- Make notes on the chart about what you find.

Useful websites or CD-ROMs	Information

NOW TRY THIS!

- Use the information you found to help you write a paragraph about the topic you chose.

Teachers' note The pupils will need access to the Internet and CD-ROMs. Before beginning, discuss the usefulness of reading a text quickly to find out what each part is about and whether it contains relevant information. The pupils should make a note of the most useful parts of the texts. During the plenary session, they could compare their key words and decide which were the most useful.

Developing Literacy
Text Level
Year 7
© A & C BLACK **15**

Make a note
STARTER

- Read the passage. Underline the words and phrases which will help you to answer the question 'What was remarkable about the Buddha?'

Who was the Buddha?

The Buddha was a man named Siddhartha Gautama who lived in northern India nearly 2,500 years ago. He is famous as the spiritual inspiration and founder of the religious path known today as Buddhism. 'Buddha' is actually a title and not a proper name. It means someone who is awakened or enlightened to the nature of life and its meaning. The title is given in recognition of this supreme spiritual attainment.

The Buddha lived from approximately 563–483 BCE (scholars dispute the dates). He is said to have been born on the full moon day of May in Terai, northern India, in the foothills of the Himalayas, near to what we now call Nepal. He led a privileged life from birth, but felt drawn to learn of spiritual truths after recognising the suffering that accompanies life. He therefore left his beloved young wife and new son, his wealth and prestige, to follow the established tradition of asceticism (renunciation, or self-denial).

Siddhartha was given the title of 'Buddha' at the age of 35 when, after six years of spiritual practices, he became enlightened to the truth behind all appearances. From the time of his enlightenment Siddhartha Gautama, the Buddha, also became known as 'Sakyamuni', the sage or wise teacher of the Sakya people from whom he came, although he preferred the term 'Tathagata' (Truthsayer). Siddhartha saw how suffering is caused by ignorance and desire, and how ignorance can be removed. After his enlightenment he no longer clung to existence or to the idea that he had any eternal essence or identity. The Buddha began to teach out of compassion for the suffering of those not yet enlightened to the truth of all things. He travelled widely for 45 years, teaching others how to reach the same understanding and insight. He died at the age of 80. His last words are recorded in many reference works as: 'All created things are perishable; work diligently on your own salvation.'

From *Buddha: A Beginner's Guide* by Gillian Stokes

Teachers' note Photocopy this page onto an OHT. Model how to prepare for taking notes by skimming the first paragraph and stopping at words or phrases which suggest what was remarkable about the Buddha. Underline these words and ask the pupils if they know why you have done so. Encourage them to join in skimming the second paragraph and to suggest which words to underline. Point out that when reading books, the pupils must not underline words, but they can write on sticky notes or slips of paper and use these to mark the pages.

16

Developing Literacy
Text Level
Year 7
© A & C BLACK

Make a note

- Make notes using the underlined words and phrases from the passage about the Buddha. Write your notes on the chart.

When you write notes, miss out unimportant words like 'a' and 'the'. You can shorten words, use initial letters and miss out letters.

The question I am trying to answer:

What was remarkable about the Buddha?

Notes

What was remarkable about his background

What he did that was remarkable

What was remarkable about the way other people treated him

Useful abbreviations

approx	approximately
b	born
b/c	because
BCE	Before the Common Era
d	died
est	established
ID	identity
ign	ignorance
insp	inspiration
n	north/northern
prac	practice
rec	recognition
s'tual	spiritual
t'chr	teacher
yr	year

Useful symbols

+	and
∴	therefore
↓	down
→	to, towards
↑	up

NOW TRY THIS!

- Use your notes to help you write a paragraph to answer the question 'What was remarkable about the Buddha?' Do not look at the original passage about the Buddha.

Teachers' note The pupils will need to refer to the completed starter activity. Point out that making notes enables them to write information in their own words, rather than copying from a text. Discuss that it saves time if they take notes only of the information they need. The pupils should not abbreviate words they need to practise spelling, such as *Buddha* and *Siddhartha Gautama*.

Developing Literacy
Text Level
Year 7
© A & C BLACK   **17**

Web versus books

∘STARTER

This is the opening page of the 'daily diet' section of the government's Food Standards Agency website. You can move to another page by clicking on any of the underlined text.

• Describe how you would use the website to find the answer to a question about daily diet.

Your daily diet
This section provides information on your daily diet including nutrient groups, fruit and veg, meat, fish and eggs, dairy products, bread and cereals and fats and sugars.

Remember that the key to a healthy diet is to eat a variety of foods, which for most people means eating:

○ more fruit and veg
○ more bread, cereals and potatoes
○ less fat and sugar

Find out **more**

Bread and cereals
Aim to eat lots of these sorts of foods, which should make up about a third of your diet. <u>More</u>

Fruit and veg
Most people know that we should be eating more fruit and veg. But most of us still aren't eating enough. Did you know that we should be eating at least five portions of fruit and veg every day? <u>More</u>

Meat, fish, eggs and pulses
For most people, a healthy diet means eating only moderate amounts of meat, fish and alternatives such as pulses, eggs, nuts and beans, and choosing lower fat versions when you can. <u>More</u>

Fats and sugars
A healthy diet means eating and drinking less of these sorts of foods. <u>More</u>

Dairy foods
For a healthy diet, most people should eat dairy foods such as milk, cheese, yoghurt and fromage frais in moderate amounts. If you want to cut down on fat, choose lower fat versions whenever you can. <u>More</u>

Salt: are you getting too much?
We all need to eat some salt, but most of us are eating too much. Salt is present naturally in food and we also use it to flavour and preserve foods. <u>More</u>

See **also**

○ <u>Nutrition research</u>

Search site
  GO

FOOD DIRECTORY A–Z

Ask an expert...

Can kiwi fruit cause an allergic reaction?

Answer...

TODAY'S FEATURES

SAFE SUMMER SIZZLING
<u>Top tips</u>
<u>Silly burger quiz</u>

TOP SEARCHES
<u>Publications</u>
<u>Salt</u>
<u>Jobs</u>
<u>Meat</u>
<u>Food poisoning</u>

FOOD INTOLERANCE
<u>What causes it?</u>
<u>Treatments</u>
<u>FAQs</u>
<u>What we're doing</u>

INDUSTRY GUIDANCE
<u>Additives</u>
<u>Basmati</u>
<u>Origin labelling</u>
<u>Meat cutting</u>

CYMRAEG/
WELSH LANGUAGE

ARCHIVE

DIET AND HEALTH
<u>Vitamins and minerals</u>
<u>Food intolerance</u>
<u>Advice for you</u>
<u>Food and weight</u>
<u>Your daily diet</u>
<u>Food myths debunked</u>
<u>Food-related conditions</u>
<u>Ask an expert</u>
<u>Fifty years of food</u>

Adapted from the Food Standards Agency website

Teachers' note Split the class into small groups and give each group a copy of this page. Before the lesson, each group should prepare a question on daily diet. You could begin by discussing the ways in which the pupils use the Internet for research. Stress that if they print out web pages indiscriminately, they end up using websites as if they were books. Allow them five minutes to discuss how they would use the website to answer their question, then invite them to share their ideas. Discuss that many different routes through the website could prove useful.

Developing Literacy
Text Level
Year 7
© A & C BLACK

Web versus books

- Use a website to find the answer to a question about daily diet. You could go to:

  www.foodstandards.gov.uk/healthiereating/dailydiet/

- Use a book to find the answer to the same question.
- Record on the chart what you did and what you found out.

Spend the same amount of time using the website and the book.

!

My question: _____

How I used the source		
	Website	**Book**
Step 1		
Step 2		
Step 3		
Step 4		

What I found out	
Website	**Book**

NOW TRY THIS!

- Write a report comparing how books and websites are used. Write about the advantages and disadvantages of each, including the ways in which one is easier or quicker than the other.

Teachers' note The pupils will need access to books about healthy living which include dietary advice. They could work in pairs to look for answers to the same question – one using a book and the other using a website. Ask them to set a suitable time limit for their research. At the end of the time limit they can compare their findings and complete the chart together.

Be an active reader
STARTER

• Read the passage. What do you 'see' as you read each paragraph? Make notes on the notepad about what you find out.

Stanley Yelnats was the only passenger on the bus, not counting the driver or the guard. The guard sat next to the driver with his seat turned around facing Stanley. A rifle lay across his lap.

Stanley was sitting about ten rows back, handcuffed to his armrest. His backpack lay on the seat next to him. It contained his toothbrush, toothpaste, and a box of stationery his mother had given him. He'd promised to write to her at least once a week.

He looked out the window, although there wasn't much to see – mostly fields of hay and cotton. He was on a long bus ride to nowhere. The bus wasn't air-conditioned, and the hot, heavy air was almost as stifling as the handcuffs.

Stanley and his parents had tried to pretend that he was just going away to camp for a while, just like rich kids do. When Stanley was younger he used to play with stuffed animals, and pretend the animals were at camp. Camp Fun and Games he called it. Sometimes he'd have them play soccer with a marble. Other times they'd run an obstacle course, or go bungee jumping off a table, tied to broken rubber bands. Now Stanley tried to pretend he was going to Camp Fun and Games. Maybe he'd make some friends, he thought. At least he'd get to swim in the lake.

He didn't have any friends at home. He was overweight and the kids at his middle school often teased him about his size. Even his teachers sometimes made cruel comments without realizing it. On his last day of school, his math teacher, Mrs. Bell, taught ratios. As an example, she chose the heaviest kid in the class and the lightest kid in the class, and had them weigh themselves. Stanley weighed three times as much as the other boy. Mrs. Bell wrote the ratio on the board, 3:1, unaware of how much embarrassment she had caused both of them.

Stanley was arrested later that day.

From *Holes* by Louis Sachar

• How do you feel about Stanley?

• He has been arrested. What might have been the reason for this?

• What do you think is going to happen to him?

Teachers' note Ask the pupils to work in pairs and give each pair a copy of this page. They should discuss and agree between them what to write on the notepad. Encourage them to discuss their responses to the passage, using the questions at the foot of the page as prompts. Allow about five minutes, then invite feedback. You could ask the pupils to identify the words and phrases which make them think or feel as they do.

Developing Literacy
Text Level
Year 7
© A & C BLACK

Be an active reader

- In a novel you have read, look for a passage which appeals to your feelings about a character.
- Complete the chart. Describe how you feel about the character and why. Support your answer by quoting from the passage.

Title of book: _____ **Chapter:** _____

Author: _____ **Page:** _____

Summary of the story so far

_____
_____
_____
_____
_____

Feelings about the character	Reasons

Evidence from passage

_____
_____
_____
_____
_____

NOW TRY THIS!

- Make notes about your responses to another book you are reading. Think about how you feel about the characters.
- Explain how the author makes you feel this way.

Does the author appeal to your emotions through language or through the type of information given?

!

Teachers' note First discuss how the writer of the passage in the starter activity appeals to the reader's emotions. Point out the effect of the information given about Stanley (the disadvantages he has and how they affect him). Also remind the pupils how the narrative style contributes to this effect. Help them to choose a passage from a novel to analyse in a similar way.

Developing Literacy
Text Level
Year 7
© A & C BLACK **21**

What does it say?
STARTER

- Read the poem.

Cool Medium

In fifty-three the children up our road

Got television and disappeared indoors

After school, instead of coming out

To toast crusts over stick fires in the hedgerow

Or fill the first-starred, batwinged dusks of autumn

With clamour of wild games. I sulked around

The silent woods, refused their invitations,

And hated ever since those moon-grey flickers

From a dead planet. Now, at night, I still

Walk past curtained windows, knowing each

Conceals that strange communion. Is life

Something to be given up for that?

Amused, superior, grown-up faces smile:

The awkward child stalks in the woodland still,

Keeping the ward of long-abandoned places,

As if one day the others might come back,

Stubborn in an antique heresy,

With trees and winter stars for company.

David Sutton

- What is the poet saying about the effect of television on children? Underline the words and phrases which communicate this message.

- What is he saying about people's responses to anyone who does not conform? Use a different colour to underline the words and phrases which communicate this message.

Teachers' note Photocopy this page onto an OHT and read the poem with the class. Discuss what the poet is writing about: he begins by narrating something he remembers from his childhood, but this is not purely a narrative poem. The pupils should look for evidence that the poet is using a narrative form to communicate a message. Invite them to come and underline the significant words and phrases on the OHT.

22

Developing Literacy
Text Level
Year 7
© A & C BLACK

What does it say?

- Record on the chart the ways in which the poet communicates the messages in 'Cool Medium'.

Write the words and phrases which suggest these contrasts.

Contrasts in the poem	
Life	**Death**
clamour	
Natural	**Unnatural**
Modern	**Old-fashioned**
Sensible, sophisticated, 'normal'	**Silly, naïve, not 'normal'**

NOW TRY THIS!

- List the words and phrases in the poem which help to create a feeling of mourning or sadness.
- Despite this mournfulness, the poet suggests something hopeful. What is this and how does he suggest it?

Teachers' note The pupils will need to refer to the poem in the starter activity. During the plenary session, invite them to share their answers and encourage them to notice the rhythm and pace of the poem. Discuss how this adds to the feeling of mourning and sadness.

Who is the audience?

STARTER

- Read this passage from a magazine.

This month we've been mostly...

Winning awards. There were Cadbury's Flake cakes in the office to celebrate beauty director Charmian's Wella Hair Journalism Award. She scooped a wicked trophy and a cheque for £500, which she immediately blew in Tiffany and Gucci. You go, girl!

Having our future predicted. At the Atomic Kitten photoshoot, I accosted Rashid Ahmad, the visiting psychic. According to his tarot cards, I'm about to receive a romantic proposal. Yikes! I'll keep you posted.

Wearing sunglasses, even though it's dark. Well, they are Burberry and at £80 they're not as pricey as most designer shades. It's never too cold to be cool.

Chilling out. This month, my obsessions are smelly candles and essential oil burners. My gorgeous Origins candle lasts for weeks and one whiff leaves me relaxed and serene.

Yum!

- To what type of audience will the magazine appeal? Choose a rating between 1 and 6 for each scale and put a cross in the box.

	1	2	3	4	5	6	
Young							Old
Fun-loving							Serious
Quiet							Lively
Introvert							Extrovert
Relaxed							Tense
Traditional							Modern

- Underline the evidence in the passage. Use a different colour for each ratings choice and colour the rows of the chart to make a key.

Teachers' note Ask the pupils to work in pairs and give each pair a copy of this page. Encourage them to respond quickly; after reading the passage together, allow only one minute for them to complete the ratings chart. Invite feedback before asking them to create the colour key and mark the evidence for their responses. At the end of the session, you could discuss the register of the text (formal or informal) and the features that characterise this type of language.

Developing Literacy
Text Level
Year 7
© A & C BLACK

Who is the audience?

- Read this passage from a magazine.

In a recent office straw poll February was voted the least favourite month of the year. Festivities are a dim and distant dream, the nights are still dark, the weather can often be cold and snowy and, at present, summer seems an extremely long way off.

To banish such dull thoughts, we have, once again, been thinking up some stunning features to inform and entertain you. Our special section is on fabrics. We've been delving into the history of natural textiles such as wool and linen and have come up with some beautiful modern-day examples. If you are at the decoration stage of restoring your home, turn to page 42 for valuable expert advice on the various curtain styles suitable for traditional settings. Our choice of tie-backs and trimmings will also give you ideas for authentic and original finishing touches. If, however, your furnishings need a bit of a face-lift, discover the best ways to clean and restore them on page 54.

- Predict what kind of audience will be interested in reading the magazine.
- To explain your answer, describe the way in which the language appeals to this audience.

Our prediction: _____

_____

_____

_____

Describe the audience. Think about their age, personality and interests.

Reasons: _____

_____

_____

_____

_____

Which language features will appeal to this audience?

NOW TRY THIS!

- Plan a survey to find out what type of people would be interested in reading the magazine, and why.
- Record your findings and compare them with your prediction.

Teachers' note Ask the pupils to read the passage with a partner and to comment on whether they themselves would want to read the magazine, and why or why not. They could complete a ratings scale like the one in the starter activity for the type of audience it would appeal to.

Developing Literacy
Text Level
Year 7
© A & C BLACK **25**

Character and mood

STARTER

• Read the passage. What does it tell you about David?

David would sometimes stand in the shadows outside a shop and listen to the conversation within. It was easy enough for they always talked very loudly with frequent bursts of laughter. In that way he learnt what many things were used for, things that were strange to him but seemed to be taken for granted by the people round him.

He had not yet heard anyone talk about *them*: sometimes the fact that there were obviously none of them in the town led him to be rather less careful. He always walked on if anyone looked at him, but he sometimes came very near to forgetting his fears, and he quite openly filled his bottle at the pump down by the seafront and accepted several loaves from the man who made them. At first he would stand for a long time hidden in the shadows outside the shop listening to the baker's conversation with his customers – but it was never about *them*, and he never asked David any questions except whether he were hungry, and then he would give him a loaf and a friendly smile.

And so it was almost out of habit that David now hid in the dark outside and listened. That evening the man was talking of someone called Guglio and the good catch he had had. For a moment David's heart stood still with fear... Then he realized they were talking, not of people, but of fish caught at sea.

He stood there a little longer, in his relief forgetting to listen. Then he suddenly heard the man say, "Who's that boy that comes here every evening for a loaf? Do you know?"

"What boy?"

"A thin ragged boy, but always very clean. He looks a bit foreign."

David pressed himself flat against the wall and stood there as if glued to the spot. Another man was speaking now, one who spoke differently from the rest, more after David's own fashion, "I've seen a strange boy every evening this week: he stands and looks at the church. I assumed he'd come over for the harvest."

Then a woman said something. "No one's come yet for the harvest, padre. I've seen the boy, too. It must be the same one. He doesn't look like the others and he always moves off when you look at him. He's got very strange-looking eyes..."

"In what way strange?" – that was the one they called 'padre' speaking again: 'padre' meant 'priest' – "I've only seen him standing in the dark on the other side of the square... Does he look as if he's up to mischief?"

"No, no, I don't know about that, padre, but he's a strange boy. If you smile at him, he doesn't smile back; he doesn't run off, either; he just turns and walks away. And his eyes... they're so quiet-looking. Perhaps we should get hold of him and ask him where he comes from."

David heard no more. With no more sound than a puff of wind he was down the street and inside the first open door – through a long dark passage and out again in another street.

From *I Am David* by Anne Holm

Teachers' note Give each pupil, or each pair, a copy of this page. Read the passage with the pupils, then invite them to say what they have learned about David without referring to the passage (what he looks like, what they can deduce about his background, and what he is doing). Record their responses and ask what gave them these impressions. Return to the passage and check the evidence. Discuss how information about David is communicated: through narration of what he does, thinks and feels and through dialogue in which other people talk about him.

Developing Literacy
Text Level
Year 7
© A & C BLACK

Character and mood

- Answer these questions based on the passage from *I Am David*.

- Write an example from the passage which shows David's fear through recounting what he does.

  _____

- The writer uses contrast to emphasise David's fear. Write an example of this.

  _____

  _____

- Write examples which give the impression that David hears snatches of conversation which seem to fade away every so often.

  _____

  _____

- List three examples from the dialogue which tell you about what David looks like and how he behaves.

  _____

  _____

  _____

- Find a comparison which shows how David slipped away from the scene.

  _____

- In several sentences the writer uses **ellipses** (...). What effect does this have?

  _____

  _____

  _____

  _____

  > Try rewriting the sentences without the ellipses. Compare them with the original sentences.

NOW TRY THIS!

- Choose a passage from another book you know.
- Write about how the writer conveys character, setting and mood. Think about the way the story is told, the use of dialogue and the types of sentence structure.

Teachers' note The pupils will need to refer to the passage in the starter activity. Explain that the mood of a text is its emotional 'feel'. During the plenary session, you could ask the pupils to summarise what is revealed about David through dialogue. Ask them to explain how the passage would be different if the dialogue were replaced with a straightforward description of David.

Lively language

Tarantella

Do you remember an Inn,   1
Miranda?
Do you remember an Inn?
And the tedding and the spreading
Of the straw for a bedding,   5
And the fleas that tease in the High Pyrenees,
And the wine that tasted of the tar?
And the cheers and the jeers of the young muleteers
(Under the dark of the vine verandah)?
Do you remember an Inn, Miranda,   10
Do you remember an Inn?
And the cheers and the jeers of the young muleteers
Who hadn't got a penny,
And who weren't paying any,
And the hammer at the doors and the Din?   15
And the Hip! Hop! Hap!
Of the clap
Of the hands to the twirl and the swirl
Of the girl gone chancing,
Glancing,   20
Dancing,
Backing and advancing,
Snapping of the clapper to the spin
Out and in –
And the Ting, Tong, Tang of the guitar!   25
Do you remember an Inn,
Miranda?
Do you remember an Inn?
Never more;
Miranda,   30
Never more.
Only the high peaks hoar:
And Aragon a torrent at the door.
No sound
In the walls of the Halls where falls   35
The tread
Of the feet of the dead to the ground.
No sound:
Only the boom
Of the far Waterfall like Doom.   40

Hilaire Belloc

Teachers' note Photocopy this page onto an OHT and read the poem with the class. Ask the pupils what kinds of images and sounds are conjured up by the poem, and whether the general feel is quiet or noisy, calm or lively, sad or happy. Invite them to underline the rhyming words, then discuss the pattern of the rhyme and how it affects the rhythm and pace of the poem. You could also revise onomatopoeia and ask the pupils to look for examples; discuss how these affect the rhythm and pace of the poem.

Developing Literacy
Text Level
Year 7
© A & C BLACK

28

Lively language

- Rewrite this section of the poem 'Tarantella'. Replace the words in **bold** with | synonyms | (for instance, you could replace 'tedding' with 'scattering'). Your new words do not need to rhyme.

Synonyms are words with the same or similar meanings. Use a dictionary and a thesaurus.

Do you remember an Inn,

Miranda?

Do you remember an Inn?

And the **tedding** and the spreading

Of the straw for a **bedding**,

And the fleas that **tease** in the

    High Pyrenees,

And the wine that tasted of the tar?

And the **cheers** and the **jeers** of the

    young muleteers

(Under the dark of the vine

    verandah)?

Who hadn't got a penny,

And who weren't paying any,

And the hammer at the doors and

    the **Din**?

- Explain the difference these changes make to the rhythm and pace of the poem.

- Identify three heavy-sounding words in the slow section of the poem (lines 34–40).

NOW TRY THIS!

- Rewrite lines 34–40 of the poem. Replace the heavy-sounding words with synonyms.
- Describe the effect of these changes.

Teachers' note The pupils will need to refer to the poem in the starter activity. During the plenary session, discuss how the poet uses different rhyme patterns to set the rhythm of different parts of the poem. Also discuss the effects of the words he chooses (lively, heavy, quick, slow and so on).

A reading journal
STARTER

Reading journal for Iqbal Hussain

Title: *Wicked Words*   **Author:** Terry Deary
Publisher: Andre Deutsch   **Number of pages:** 192
Subject: Word derivations   **Fiction or non-fiction?** Non-fiction

What is this book about?

This book is a kind of history of the English language. It gives information about how English has developed and how invaders and settlers in Britain have influenced the language. It gives the derivations of words and the sources of proverbs and sayings.

For what audience is it written?

It is meant for anyone from about age ten upwards (although younger children who are good readers might enjoy it). The book doesn't say it is for this age group, but the language and ideas would be too difficult for younger children. I know it is suitable for adults, too, because I can never find mine, since my mum is always reading it. She reads parts of it aloud to my dad and he enjoys it, too.

How does it compare with other books on the same subject?

It is better than any other word-derivation books I have read because it makes the topic fun. I laugh aloud when I read it (so do my mum and dad). It uses jokes and cartoons to explain things.

Wicked Words also gives some interesting examples from Shakespeare. These make me quite look forward to reading Shakespeare at school.

My reasons for liking or disliking the book

Apart from the interesting subject and the jokes and funny stories, I liked some of the unusual derivations which most adults obviously don't know, or they wouldn't use the words. One of these is 'poppycock', which is our headteacher's favourite word for describing our excuses for not doing our homework. I bet she wouldn't use it if she knew it came from a Danish word for 'soft cow-droppings'. She tells us off when we use modern words like that!

I also like being able to use words that many adults do not know: for example, 'glabrous' (bald) and 'kippage' (a state of great excitement). I've noticed that the person who wrote the spell-checker on my PC didn't know them.

Teachers' note Photocopy this page onto an OHT and read the passage with the pupils. Ask them whether they enjoyed reading it, and draw out the idea that keeping a reading journal can be fun. Encourage the pupils to notice how the writer of the journal backs up his answers with evidence and mentions the responses of people other than himself to support his recommendation of the book. Discuss that the style of the journal is relaxed and informal, allowing the writer to present sensible ideas in a humorous way.

30

Developing Literacy
Text Level
Year 7
© A & C BLACK

A reading journal

Reading journal for _____

Title: _____ Author: _____

Publisher: _____ Number of pages: _____

Subject: _____ Fiction or non-fiction? _____

What is this book about?

_____

_____

_____

> Explain the subject of the book. Say what aspects of the subject it covers.

For what audience is it written?

_____

_____

_____

> Write how you can tell. Mention the vocabulary, style of language and level of difficulty.

How does it compare with other books on the same subject?

_____

_____

_____

> Explain how this book is better or worse than others you have read.

My reasons for liking or disliking the book

_____

_____

_____

_____

_____

> Write about your personal response to the book. Make sure you give sensible reasons for your opinions.

Teachers' note Ask the pupils to complete the journal page for a book they have recently read. They may find it helpful to refer to the example in the starter activity. Discuss with the pupils the characteristics of different types of writing and, if necessary, help them to recognise the type and genre of books they have read.

Developing Literacy
Text Level
Year 7
© A & C BLACK **31**

Fit forms

STARTER

- Read the haikus.
- Count the number of | syllables | in each line. Does this match what you already know about haikus?
- In what ways is the haiku form suitable for this subject matter?

> Remember, a syllable is a sound unit of a word. Syllables give the poem its rhythm.

!

Art Year Haikus   **Syllables**

Spring morning sun bathes   Line 1 ☐

Pink blossom and brave, bright birds.   Line 2 ☐

I take out my paints.   Line 3 ☐   Total ☐

Summer sun has come.   Line 1 ☐

Fields of corn are gay with gold.   Line 2 ☐

I paint before rain.   Line 3 ☐   Total ☐

One bold rose remains   Line 1 ☐

Despite night's slight bite of frost.   Line 2 ☐

I'll save it in paint.   Line 3 ☐   Total ☐

All is dressed in snow.   Line 1 ☐

A fox pads across tight ice,   Line 2 ☐

His brush caught by mine.   Line 3 ☐   Total ☐

John Kitching

Teachers' note Photocopy this page onto an OHT. First read the haikus with the pupils and revise what they have already learned about haikus. Encourage them to find out more from a dictionary, encyclopedia or other reference book. Revise syllables (see page 64) and suggest that the pupils tap out the syllables if they need to. They should say what they notice about the rhythm and pace of the haikus and the resulting mood. Draw out how the third line of each haiku is different in sense from the first two lines, and how the last haiku is slightly different in tone from the others.

Developing Literacy
Text Level
Year 7
© A & C BLACK

Fit forms

• Use the chart below to help you plan a haiku.

Subject of haiku	
Title	

Ideas to include	Vocabulary which will help to create the right mood

Line 1
Line 2
Line 3

The subject should be connected with nature.

Make notes about your ideas.

Try out some lines, count the **syllables** and adjust them.

The last line should add an interesting or surprising twist.

!

• Edit your haiku and write the final version.

• Read other haikus. Write a description of the way in which the haiku form helps to create a particular rhythm and pace.

Teachers' note Encourage the pupils to create a smooth, calm rhythm which is appropriate for the subject matter. They should focus at first on the ideas and impressions they want to communicate rather than the number of syllables; this can be adjusted afterwards. For the extension activity, ensure that further examples of haikus are available for the pupils to read.

A perfect plan

STARTER

- Cut out the paragraphs.
- Rearrange them in the correct order.
- With a partner, summarise the information you find in each paragraph. What plan can you see in the passage?

Trooping the colour

The colour that is 'trooped' before the Queen today is the regimental colour of a Foot Guard battalion. The troops (soldiers) involved are part of the Household Division of the Army, which is traditionally responsible for guarding the monarch. Since only one colour may be trooped at the parade, the five regiments take turns year by year. The spectacular event is watched by millions worldwide.

In 1748 it was decided that this parade would also mark the monarch's official birthday. During the reign of Edward VII (1901–1910), it became the custom for the monarch to take the salute in person at the ceremony.

Perhaps you have seen on television the parade called 'trooping the colour' and wondered what it was all about? This colourful parade takes place on the Queen's official birthday.

At one time trooping the colour was carried out almost every day. Those were the days when regimental colours (the flags of the battalions) were carried into battle and served as a guide and rallying point for the soldiers. So it was important for every soldier to be familiar with his own regimental colours. These were therefore regularly carried ('trooped') down the ranks of soldiers in peacetime.

Teachers' note Ask the pupils to work in pairs and give each pair a copy of this page. Encourage them to discuss how the author has planned the text, then bring together their findings. Draw their attention to the connectives (linking words) which join the ideas of different paragraphs. They should notice that there is an introduction which sets the scene, followed by an explanation, further clarification and a conclusion which relates the topic back to the present day. Discuss that the purpose of the text is to communicate information, so the plan needs to be simple and direct.

Developing Literacy
Text Level
Year 7
© A & C BLACK

A perfect plan

• Make notes on these formats for a text you are going to write.

Topic: _____

Format 1

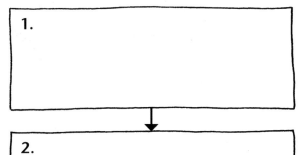

1.

↓

2.

↓

3.

↓

4.

↓

5.

Format 2

1.

2.

Write the main point or idea here.

3.

4.

• Discuss with a partner which format is better for planning different kinds of writing.

Think about text-types such as reports, explanations, instructions and discussions.

!

NOW TRY THIS!

• Read a chapter from a history or geography book on a topic you are studying.
• Make notes for a report on the topic. Plan your report using a suitable format.

Teachers' note This page can be used to plan a piece of writing in English or another subject. Explain that one format may be more useful than the other, depending on the text-type. You could demonstrate this using a plan of the passage in the starter activity. For the extension activity, the pupils could draw their own planning format or use another copy of the sheet.

**Developing Literacy
Text Level
Year 7**
© A & C BLACK **35**

Structure it
STARTER

• Read this opening of a science fiction story.

How do you know it is an opening?

What is good about it as the start of a story?

What information does it give you? What else would you like to know?

How do you think the story will continue?

The Star Beast

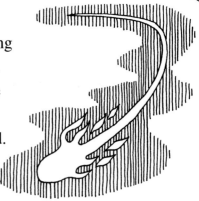

Soon upon a time, and not so far ahead, there was a long streak of light down the night sky, a flicker of fire, and a terrible bang that startled all who heard it, even those who were normally inured to noise. When day came, the matter was discussed, argued, and finally dismissed. For no one could discover any cause at all for the disturbance.

Shortly afterwards, at a farm, there was heard a scrabbling at the door, and a crying. When the people went to see what was there, they found a creature. It was not easy to tell what sort of creature, but far too easy to tell that it was hurt and hungry and afraid. Only its pain and hunger had brought it to the door for help.

Being used to beasts, the farmer and his wife tended the thing. They put it in a loose-box and tended it. They brought water in a big basin and it drank thirstily, but with some difficulty – for it seemed to want to lift it to his mouth instead of lapping, and the basin was too big, and it was too weak. So it lapped. The farmer dressed the great burn that seared its thigh and shoulder and arm. He was kind enough, in a rough way, but the creature moaned, and set its teeth, and muttered strange sounds, and clenched its front paws…

From *Mainly in Moonlight* by Nicholas Stuart Grey

Teachers' note Split the class into small groups and give each group a copy of this page. Read the passage with the pupils and explain anything they find difficult, then give each group one of the four questions to discuss. After five minutes the groups should report back to the rest of the class, supporting their answers with evidence where appropriate. Discuss that good story openings provide information but also interest the reader in what is going to happen next. Ask the pupils to consider whether the 'creature' in the story could in fact be a human being.

Developing Literacy
Text Level
Year 7
© A & C BLACK

Structure it

- Use this page to help you structure a short story. Make notes on the chart.

The **genre** could be science fiction, fantasy, mystery, adventure, historical fiction…

Title:	Genre:
Characters	**Location**
What will the story be about?	**How will you begin the story?**
What complication will there be?	**How will this reach a crisis?**
What impact will the crisis have on the characters?	**How will you resolve the crisis to give a satisfying ending?**

- Write your story.

Remember:
- ☆ the opening should interest readers and make them want to read on
- ☆ develop the plot and include a complication
- ☆ to finish the story, tie up loose ends and perhaps leave readers with something to think about.

Teachers' note The pupils could use the science fiction story opening in the starter activity as the basis of their own short story. Encourage them to use their experience of television, film and literature to resolve the story in a 'happy-ever-after' or sad ending. During the plenary session, discuss the effect of different story endings.

Create a character
STARTER

- Read these character descriptions by Charles Dickens.
- Underline the adjectives in each passage. Discuss how the adjectives reveal Dickens' attitude towards the characters.
- In a different colour, underline what the characters do. Discuss what these actions tell you about the characters.

Do you think Dickens likes each character? How can you tell?

Mrs Gamp

She was a fat old woman this Mrs Gamp, with a husky voice and a moist eye which she had a remarkable power of turning up, and only showing the white of it. Having very little neck, it cost her some trouble to look over herself, if one may say so, at those to whom she talked. She wore a very rusty black gown, rather the worse for snuff, and a shawl and a bonnet to correspond. The face of Mrs Gamp – the nose in particular – was somewhat red and swollen, and it was difficult to enjoy her society without becoming conscious of a smell of spirits.

From *Martin Chuzzlewit* by Charles Dickens

Miss Murdstone

It was Miss Murdstone who was arrived, and a gloomy-looking lady she was; dark, like her brother, whom she greatly resembled in face and voice, and with very heavy eyebrows, nearly meeting over her large nose, as if, being disabled by the wrongs of her sex from wearing whiskers, she had carried them to that account. She brought with her two uncompromising hard black boxes, with her initials on the lids in hard brass nails. When she paid the coachman she took her money out of a hard steel purse, and she kept the purse in a very jail of a bag which hung upon her arm by a heavy chain, and shut up like a bite. I had never, at that time, seen such a metallic lady altogether as Miss Murdstone was.

From *David Copperfield* by Charles Dickens

Teachers' note Photocopy this page onto an OHT. Read the passages with the class and discuss how the characters are portrayed. The pupils should realise that the adjectives are emotive as well as factual and so reveal the writer's attitude. Model how the author could have chosen other words, and discuss what the effect of these would be. Develop this by talking about the other ways in which a writer can portray character, through what they say and do. The choice of a character's name can also indicate the author's attitude.

Developing Literacy
Text Level
Year 7
© A & C BLACK

Create a character

- Choose a character in a story you are writing.
- Make notes on the chart to help you plan a description of the character.

Use adjectives to describe particular features of the character. How will your choice of adjectives reveal your feelings towards him or her?

!

Name of character: _____

What the character looks like	How the character behaves
	What this shows about his or her personality
What the character says	**A situation in which the character reveals what he or she is really like**
What this shows about his or her personality	

- Imagine your character went missing and the police were searching for him or her. Write a description for the police to use in their search.

Include the same kind of detail, but think about the different purpose and audience. How will the style change?

Teachers' note Remind the pupils about the importance of considering audience and purpose. When writing fiction, the author may reveal his or her feelings about a character, but in a factual description emotive language should not be used: for instance, *his dark, greasy hair hung in long, lifeless strands* is a suitable description for fictional writing but not for a police report.

Said and done

STARTER

- Read the passage.
- First list what the character does.
- Discuss what impression of Long John Silver this gives.
- Now list what the character says, and what others say and think about him.
- Discuss what impression of Long John Silver this gives.

Long John Silver

Aboard ship he carried a crutch by a lanyard round his neck, to have both hands as free as possible. It was something to see him wedge the foot of the crutch against the bulkhead, and, propped against it, yielding to every movement of the ship, get on with his cooking like someone safe ashore. Still more strange was it to see him in the heaviest of weather cross the deck. He had a line or two rigged up to help him across the widest spaces – and he would hand himself from one place to another, now using the crutch, now trailing it alongside by the lanyard, as quickly as another man could walk. Yet some of the men who had sailed with him before expressed their pity to see him so reduced.

'He's no common man,' said the coxswain to me. 'He had good schooling in his young days, and he can speak like a book when so minded; and brave, a lion's nothing alongside of Long John! I seen him grapple four, and knock their heads together – him unharmed.'

All the crew respected and even obeyed him. He had a way of talking to each, and doing everybody some particular service. To me he was kind; and always glad to see me in the galley, which he kept as clean as a new pin; the dishes hanging up burnished, with his parrot in a cage in one corner.

'Come away, Hawkins,' he would say; 'come and have a yarn with John. Nobody more welcome than yourself, my son. Sit you down and hear the news. Here's Cap'n Flint – I calls my parrot Cap'n Flint, after the famous buccaneer.'

And the parrot would say, with great rapidity, 'Pieces of eight! Pieces of eight!' till John threw his handkerchief over the cage.

From *Treasure Island* by Robert Louis Stevenson

Teachers' note The pupils should first complete the activity on pages 38–39. Split the class into groups and give each group a copy of this page. Read the passage with the whole class, dramatising it as much as possible, and discuss any difficult vocabulary (such as *lanyard* – cord). Invite the pupils to share their immediate reactions to the character, then ask them to tackle the questions in groups. At the end of the session, ask whether any of the pupils have changed their minds about the character.

Developing Literacy
Text Level
Year 7
© A & C BLACK

Said and done

- Choose a fictional character from a book, film or television programme: for example, Tracy Beaker or Harry Potter.
- Use this page to help you plan a new passage about the character.

Name of character: _____

Situation	Other characters involved
What the character says, and how	**What the character does, and how**
What this proves about his or her character	**What this proves about his or her character**

What other characters say and think about him or her

- Write the passage.

- Think about how you could portray the character differently (for example, so that you turn a hero into a villain).
- Rewrite the passage.

You will need to adapt:
- ☆ what the character says, and how
- ☆ what the character does, and how
- ☆ what others say and think about the character.

Teachers' note Emphasise the control an author has over what is revealed to the reader about the characters, and the way in which this is done. During the plenary session, discuss how easy it is to change a character from a sympathetic one to an unsympathetic one, by using different language and by changing the way in which other characters respond to him or her.

Shape and sound

STARTER

Experiment with visual and sound effects

• Read the poem. How is it different from other poems?

The Shape of a Poem

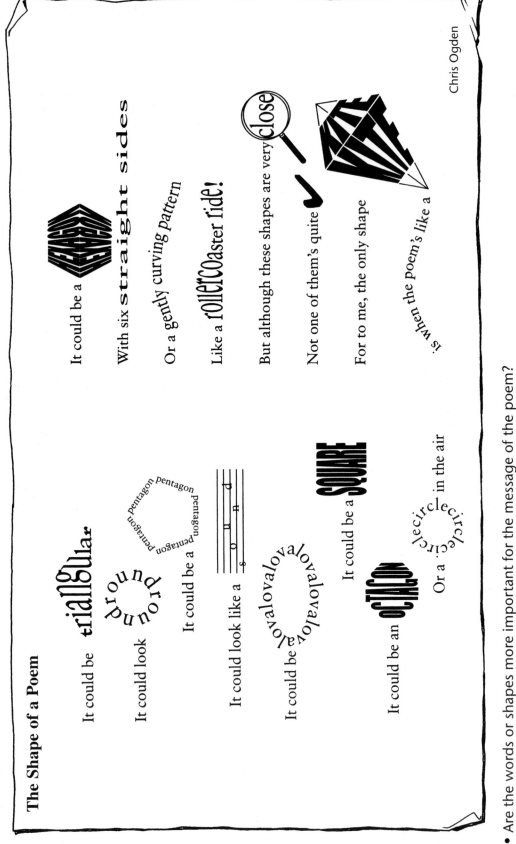

It could be   tri**a**ngular

It could look   a
               r   r
              o   o
               u   u
                 nd

It could be a   pentagon pentagon
               pentagon   pentagon
                 pentagon pentagon

It could look like a $\frac{s \quad o \quad u \quad n \quad d}{}$

It could be ovalovalovalovalovalovalovalovalovaloval

It could be a **SQUARE**

It could be an **OCTAGON**

Or a circlecirclecircle in the air

It could be a

With six **straight sides**

Or a gently curving pattern

Like a rollercoaster ride!

But although these shapes are very close

Not one of them's quite

For to me, the only shape

is when the poem's like a

Chris Ogden

• Are the words or shapes more important for the message of the poem?
• Write other words in appropriate shapes.

Teachers' note Photocopy this page onto an OHT. Read the poem with the class and discuss how the poet has experimented with word shapes and type styles to create a poem which combines visual and sound effects. Talk about whether any of the word shapes work better than others, and why. Encourage the pupils to experiment with writing words in appropriate shapes and invite them to write their ideas on the board (they could try the names of fruits or natural features such as mountains, rivers and waves).

42

Developing Literacy
Text Level
Year 7
© A & C BLACK

Shape and sound

- Read this poem. Think about the ways in which it uses shape and sound to create an effect.

Electric Guitars

I like electric guitars:
played mellow or moody,
frantic or fast – on CDs
or tapes, at home or in
cars – live in the streets,
at gigs or in bars.
    I like
    electric
    guitars:
    played
    choppy
    like
    reggae
    or angry
    like
    rock or
    chirpy
    like
    jazz or
    strummy
    like
    pop or
    heavy
    like
    metal – it
bothers me not.
I like electric guitars:
their strings and their straps
and their wild wammy bars – their
jangling and twanging and funky
wah-wahs – their fuzz boxes,
frets and multi-effects –
pick-ups, machine
heads, mahogany necks
– their plectrums, their wires,
and big amplifiers. I like electric
guitars: played loudly, politely – dully
or brightly – daily or nightly – badly
or nicely. I like electric guitars:
bass, lead and rhythm –
I basically dig 'em –
I like electric guitars

James Carter

- Find examples of | alliteration | in the poem. List them here.

  mellow or moody

- Find examples of | onomatopoeia | in the poem. List them here.

  choppy,

- Write some lines of your own about the music of electric guitars.

Alliteration is the repetition of a letter or sound at the beginning of words.

Onomatopoeia is when a word makes the sound it describes (for example, whoosh).

NOW TRY THIS!

- Write your own shape poem of an animal (such as a snake). Make the shape on the page like the shape of the animal. Use alliteration and onomatopoeia to imitate the sound and movement of the animal.

Which letters or sounds do you most associate with the animal? Which words describe the creature or the sound it makes?

Teachers' note For the extension activity, encourage the pupils to choose an animal that has a distinctive shape and makes a particular sound (a snake is ideal). During the plenary session, talk about the effects that can be achieved with shape poems, and whether this kind of approach would be unsuitable in any cases.

Organise it
STARTER

- Read this passage from a history book.
- Identify the text-type and the features of this kind of writing. Complete the chart.

Clothes in ancient Rome

The national dress of the Romans was the toga, worn over a tunic, and it was the right of all free-born citizens to wear it. Although stately, it was also cumbersome, and only the leisured upper-classes would have worn it for any length of time. Working people preferred a simple tunic, which is why the Roman historian Tacitus wrote of the 'tunic-clad populace'. Important Roman officials wore a toga with a purple stripe. The same distinctive marking was shown on the togas of boys up to the age of sixteen. At that age the youth assumed the plain *toga virilis*, dedicating his childhood garb to the household gods at a ceremony that marked an important stage in his upbringing.

An alternative form of cloak was the *pallium*, the Roman version of the Greek *himation*. During the Republic, however, this garment was frowned upon by those who thought Greek dress un-Roman and unmanly. The great general Scipio, who defeated the Carthaginians, is said to have been censured for sporting a *pallium* and sandals in the gymnasium in Sicily.

The *palla* was a garment worn by women and consisted of a deep rectangular shawl of woollen material draped around the shoulders and often drawn over the head. Together with the *stola*, a loose-fitting tunic, it constituted the traditional dress of Roman women.

From *Greek and Roman Life* by Ian Jenkins

Text-type: _____

Verbs		Style
Tense	Person	Level of formality and how you can tell
Active or passive, or a mixture		
How the information is organised		Type of audience and how you can tell

Teachers' note Photocopy this page onto an OHT and read the passage with the pupils. Then invite them to contribute to the completion of the chart. Most factual reports use the present tense, but this is a historical report, so it uses the past tense. The writing is formal in style so the use of the first and second persons (*I/we/you*) is not appropriate. Both active and passive verbs are used. The report starts with a generalisation and then goes on to describe in detail – each paragraph taking a different aspect of the Roman dress.

Developing Literacy
Text Level
Year 7
© A & C BLACK

Organise it

- Read the passage. Where would you find this type of report?

_____

- The passage is a | non-chronological | report. Make notes in the boxes about the features of this text-type.

> **!** A non-chronological report is *not* organised according to a time sequence.

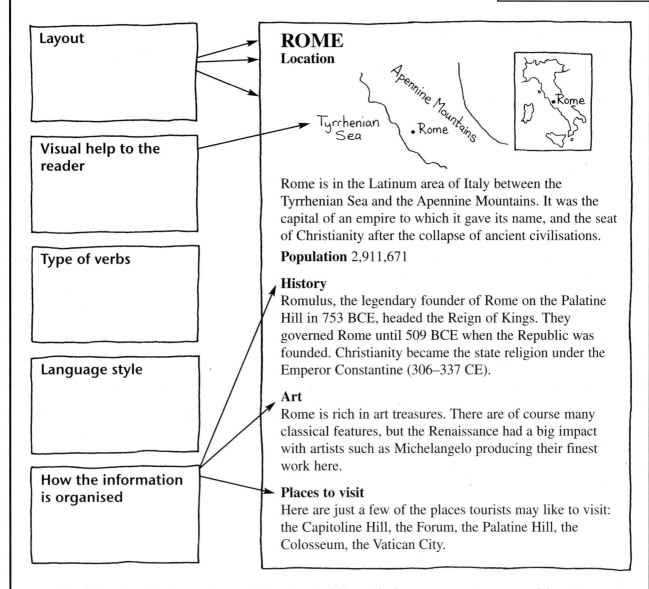

Layout

Visual help to the reader

Type of verbs

Language style

How the information is organised

ROME
Location

Tyrrhenian Sea *Apennine Mountains* *Rome* *Rome*

Rome is in the Latinum area of Italy between the Tyrrhenian Sea and the Apennine Mountains. It was the capital of an empire to which it gave its name, and the seat of Christianity after the collapse of ancient civilisations.

Population 2,911,671

History
Romulus, the legendary founder of Rome on the Palatine Hill in 753 BCE, headed the Reign of Kings. They governed Rome until 509 BCE when the Republic was founded. Christianity became the state religion under the Emperor Constantine (306–337 CE).

Art
Rome is rich in art treasures. There are of course many classical features, but the Renaissance had a big impact with artists such as Michelangelo producing their finest work here.

Places to visit
Here are just a few of the places tourists may like to visit: the Capitoline Hill, the Forum, the Palatine Hill, the Colosseum, the Vatican City.

- Explain why this type of report is set out differently from a report you would write at school.

_____

_____

NOW TRY THIS!

- Write an entry for a guidebook describing a town or city you know well. Use the style and features of a non-chronological report.

> You could choose a town or city near where you live.

Teachers' note Encourage the pupils to consider how the structure of the report is suitable for its audience and purpose. For the extension activity, the pupils should choose a place familiar to them (it need not be a tourist destination). They could use encyclopedias or the Internet to research the features of the town or city.

Developing Literacy
Text Level
Year 7
© A & C BLACK **45**

Make it clear

STARTER

- Read the information about how to make a jack-o'-lantern.
- What are the features of this text-type?

Look at the type of verbs and how the information is organised.

How to make a jack-o'-lantern for Hallowe'en

You will need:
a large, ripe pumpkin • kitchen knife • spoon • felt-tip pen • craft knife • lino tool • twigs for hair • knitting needle • night-light candle

WARNING: Take care when using knives.

Tip: You can make tasty soup from the flesh and the seeds can be roasted in the oven.

1. Cut off the top of the pumpkin using a kitchen knife. Scoop out the flesh and seeds with a spoon. Draw a face on the pumpkin with a felt-tip pen.

2. Cut out the eyes, nose and mouth with a craft knife. Use a lino tool for other details, such as eyebrows and cheeks.

3. Make holes in the top of the pumpkin with a knitting needle. Push twigs into the holes to make hair.

Tip: Make sure you have an adult with you when you light the candle.

4. Place a night-light candle inside the pumpkin to create a spooky glow. Never put the hair back on once the candle is lit. Take care when using matches and do not leave the lantern unattended.

Teachers' note Photocopy this page onto an OHT and read the instructions with the pupils. Discuss that instruction texts normally have a goal or aim (which is often stated in the title) followed by a list of materials or requirements needed to achieve this. The instructions should be a series of logical and sequential steps, perhaps helped by diagrams. The verbs are mainly in the imperative (command) form and the present tense is used.

Developing Literacy
Text Level
Year 7
© A & C BLACK

Make it clear

• Look carefully at this map. It shows tourist features around the river Thames.

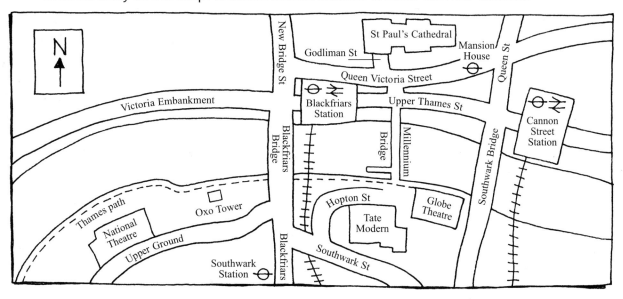

• Write directions for walking from Southwark Station to St Paul's Cathedral, calling at the Tate Modern on the way.

_____

_____

_____

_____

_____

_____

• Write directions for walking from St Paul's Cathedral to the National Theatre.

_____

_____

_____

_____

_____

_____

_____

NOW TRY THIS!

• Challenge a partner to give you directions from one place to another on the map.

• Draw a line with a pencil, following exactly the directions you are given.

• Discuss with your partner any problems you face.

• Swap roles and repeat the activity.

Teachers' note Remind the pupils that directions need to be clear and direct, so they should use imperative verb forms (such as *walk, take, continue*) and follow a logical sequence. The pupils may find it useful to number the points to highlight this. Encourage them to use connectives which give a sense of time: for example, *first, then, finally.*

Describe in detail
STARTER

• Look at these diagrams from a biology textbook.

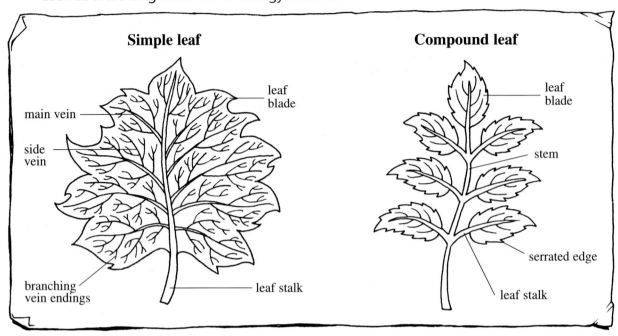

Simple leaf

leaf blade

main vein

side vein

branching vein endings

leaf stalk

Compound leaf

leaf blade

stem

serrated edge

leaf stalk

• Write descriptions of a beech leaf and a horse chestnut leaf for a science project.
Use the information and vocabulary above.

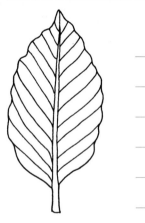

beech leaf

_____

_____

_____

_____

_____

_____

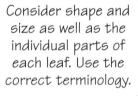

Consider shape and size as well as the individual parts of each leaf. Use the correct terminology.

horse chestnut leaf

_____

_____

_____

_____

_____

_____

_____

Teachers' note Photocopy this page onto an OHT. Explain that when giving descriptions, the pupils need to bear in mind the audience and purpose, and use appropriate language. In science, objects should be described using technical vocabulary and each part of the object should be studied in detail. Ask the pupils to describe the leaves; write their responses on the OHT. Ensure they realise that emotional language is not appropriate in this context: for example, they should not say *the leaf has an elegant shape and the veins make a pretty pattern*.

Developing Literacy
Text Level
Year 7
© A & C BLACK

Describe in detail

- Think about the shapes, colours, smells, textures and sounds of autumn leaves.
- Make notes to help you plan a description of autumn leaves for a story.

Shapes
star-shaped
jagged

Colours
golden
flaming orange

What do they smell like?
mouldy
earthy

What do they feel like?
sticky
rough

Sounds they make
crackle
whisper

- Write your description.

Use powerful adjectives and **similes** to create a vivid impression. **!**

NOW TRY THIS!

- Choose an animal, such as a spider. Write two descriptions of it:
  (a) for a science textbook
  (b) for a piece of fictional writing.
- Write about the differences between the two descriptions. Consider the purpose of each description, its audience and the impact of the vocabulary.

Teachers' note First discuss how the type of language will differ from that used in the starter activity: for example, a scientific description should not read *the flaming orange leaf fell into a myriad of fragments as I gently moved it to the microscope...* and a story would not contain descriptions such as *the side veins come from a main vein...* Revise similes and other comparisons (see page 64).

People and places
STARTER

- Read the passage. The author is describing his first night in Spain, near the city of Vigo, when at the age of 19 he set out to make his way in the world.
- Which words do you think would best fill the gaps? Choose from the lists below.
- Give reasons for your choices.

I'd known nothing then but the ⒜_____ surfaces of England, and Vigo struck me like an apparition. It seemed to rise from the sea like some ⒝_____ wreck, as old and bleached as the rocks around it. There was no smoke or movement among the houses. Everything looked barnacled, ⒞_____, and deathly quiet, as though awaiting the return of the flood…

The Galician night came quickly, the hills turned purple and the valleys ⒟_____ with shadow. The jagged coastline below, now dark and glittering, looked like sweepings of ⒠_____. Vigo was cold and dim, an unlighted ruin, already smothered in the dead ⒡_____ dusk. Only the sky and the ocean stayed alive, running with immense ⒢_____ of flame. Then as the sun went down it seemed to ⒣_____ the whole sky with it like ⒤_____ of a burning curtain, leaving rags of bright water that went on smoking and ⒥_____ along the estuaries and around the many islands. I saw the small white ship, my last link with home, ⒦_____ like a taper and die away in the darkness; then I was alone at last, sitting on a hilltop, my teeth chattering as the night wind rose.

From *As I Walked Out One Midsummer Morning* by Laurie Lee

A	B	C	D	E
barren	horrible	rotting	filled	ashes
rougher	rust-corroded	salty	flooded	broken glass
smoother	soggy	wet	suffocated	iron filings

F	G	H	I	J	K
blue	colour	drag	bits	burning	burn
dark	flares	swallow	hems	moving	flare
sinister	streams	take	shreds	smouldering	wave

Teachers' note Ask the pupils to work in pairs and give each pair a copy of this page. Read the passage with the whole class, then ask them to decide in pairs which words best suit the mood of the piece and to write them in the gaps. Invite feedback, encouraging the pupils to explain why they chose the words they did. Discuss how the author uses imagery to add to the description of the setting.

Developing Literacy
Text Level
Year 7
© A & C BLACK

People and places

- Read this passage. The mouse and his child are a clockwork toy trying to escape from Manny the Rat.
- Underline the adjectives which describe the rat.

A large rat crept out of the shadows of the girders into the light of the overhead lamps, and stood up suddenly on his hind legs before the mouse and his child. He wore a greasy scrap of silk paisley tied with a dirty string in the manner of a dressing gown, and he smelled of darkness, of stale and mouldy things, and garbage. He was there all at once and with a look of tenure, as if he had been waiting always just beyond their field of vision, and once let in would never go away. In the eerie blue glare he peered beadily at father and son, and his eyes, as passing headlights came and went, flashed blank and red like two round tiny ruby mirrors. His whiskers quivered as his face came closer; he bared his yellow teeth and smiled, and a paw shot out to strike the mouse and his child a rattling blow that knocked them flat.

From *The Mouse and His Child* by Russell Hoban

- List other information from the passage that tells us about the rat and the author's attitude towards him.

> Think about whether the rat is a hero or villain, and how you can tell. **!**

What he looks like and smells like	What he does
	crept out of the shadows

NOW TRY THIS!

- Write your own description of a villain in a story. First think of a situation in which the villain plays a part. Give details of the character's appearance, surroundings and actions. Use adjectives to help build up an impression of him or her.

> Make the character as unpleasant as possible!

Teachers' note For the extension activity, the pupils could describe a villain in a story they are writing, or in a text they are studying. During the plenary session, reinforce how the author of the passage shows his attitude towards the rat through his choice of language: for example, *crept* and *greasy*.

Persuasive power
STARTER

- Read this passage. A pig called Major is persuading other farm animals to revolt against human beings.
- Discuss how the style and content of the speech make it persuasive.

> *How does Major address the listeners? How will this make them feel?*

> *What words does Major use to describe the injustice of the animals' situation?*

> *How does the mention of Major dying make you feel?*

> *Why does he ask questions that do not require answers from the audience?*

> *Look for examples of repetition. What is the effect of this?*

Comrades, you have heard already about the strange dream that I had last night. But I will come to the dream later. I have something else to say first. I do not think, comrades, that I shall be with you for many months longer, and before I die I feel it my duty to pass on to you such wisdom as I have acquired.

Now, comrades, what is the nature of this life of ours? Let us face it, our lives are miserable, laborious and short. We are born, we are given just so much food as will keep the breath in our bodies, and those of us who are capable of it are forced to work to the last atom of our strength; and the very instant that our usefulness has come to an end we are slaughtered with hideous cruelty. No animal in England knows the meaning of happiness or leisure after he is a year old. No animal in England is free. The life of an animal is misery and slavery: that is the plain truth.

Is it not crystal clear, then, comrades, that all the evils of this life of ours spring from the tyranny of human beings? Only get rid of Man, and the produce of our labour would be our own. Almost overnight we could become rich and free. What then must we do? Why, work night and day, body and soul, for the overthrow of the human race! That is my message to you, comrades: Rebellion! I do not know when that Rebellion will come, it might be in a week or in a hundred years, but I know, as surely as I see this straw beneath my feet, that sooner or later justice will be done.

From *Animal Farm* by George Orwell

Teachers' note Split the class into groups and give each group a copy of this page. Read the passage with the whole class, then ask the groups to discuss what makes the speech persuasive, using the questions as prompts. The pupils should note down their answers along with examples from the text. Invite the groups to share their observations with the whole class; make a list of persuasive language features such as repetition and rhetorical questions.

Developing Literacy
Text Level
Year 7
© A & C BLACK

Persuasive power

- Read these opinions on whether headteachers should be allowed to cane pupils.
- Make notes on the chart about the arguments for and against.

Young people need to know that if they do something wrong there will be consequences. Caning should be the most serious form of punishment in schools.

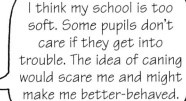
If schools involved pupils more in discussing what is right and what is wrong, there would be no need for such cruelty.

It never did me any harm when I was at school. I was always terrified of being sent to the headteacher.

I think my school is too soft. Some pupils don't care if they get into trouble. The idea of caning would scare me and might make me better-behaved.

Caning would spoil the relationship between teachers and pupils. We need to trust each other, not be terrified that our teachers will send us to be beaten.

Caning does not stop pupils from misbehaving. It's just a moment of unpleasantness which is soon forgotten. It is much better to praise and reward pupils when they behave well.

Corporal punishment is against our basic human rights. It is a form of assault.

Arguments for	Arguments against

NOW TRY THIS!

- Write a speech giving your personal view on whether caning should be allowed in schools. Use this plan to help.

Give examples and evidence to support your arguments. Use persuasive language, repetition and **rhetorical questions**.

!

① Ladies and Gentlemen, is it right that…?	② You have heard people argue that…	③ They try to justify these opinions by saying…
④ However, I believe that…	⑤ …because…	⑥ The proof is that…
⑦ I am convinced that…	⑧ Moreover,	⑨ In conclusion,

Teachers' note The pupils should summarise the views for and against caning in the appropriate columns. This will provide them with arguments to back up their personal view on the issue. They could use planning formats such as those on page 35 to plan their speech.

Rave reviews

STARTER

- Read each review. For what kind of audience is it written?
- Explain how the style is suitable for the audience: for example, slang may be used to appeal to younger readers.
- Look at the reviews one sentence at a time. Think about what each sentence is about. Work out how each review is put together.

> Are the reviews put together in different ways?

Book review

***How to be a DJ* by Janet Hoggarth**
A stylish, easy-to-read guide for the wannabe mix-wizard. You'll find out just what technical stuff you need, learn how to mix and scratch, and get hot tips from big names like Danny Rampling. First-time DJs will find plenty of reassuring advice for the big night, with FAQs to help you chill out and enjoy the vibe. Some of the technical bits might have you scratching your head, but once you've mastered the basics you're ready to have a go. Now grab a few cool choons and you're away!

☆☆☆☆☆

Video and DVD review

The Simpsons Treehouse of Horror (cert. PG)
I know what you're thinking, 'Yeah, another Simpsons compilation.' OK, this must be the umpteenth, but it's one of the best – a truly wicked collection of Hallowe'en episodes. It sends up *The Shining*, Freddy Krueger and cannibalism… it's not really scary but it will make you laugh! The only downside is that a couple of episodes don't have any twist in the tail (like the Micro-World Episode, which ends just as things start getting interesting). Essential viewing for a spooky night – but your parents won't like it!

☆☆☆☆

Teachers' note Photocopy this page onto an OHT. Read the reviews with the class and discuss the language features: for example, contractions (*can't, don't*) and use of informal language and slang expressions (*wannabe, sends up*). Discuss how this style is suitable for the audience. Then go through the reviews one sentence at a time to work out the structure: ask the pupils what each sentence is about and what its purpose is.

Developing Literacy
Text Level
Year 7
© A & C BLACK

Rave reviews

- Use this page to help you plan reviews for young people of your own age. Make notes on the charts.

Choose things to review that you have seen, read or used recently.

Review of a game, video/DVD, CD-ROM or website

Title of product or website name and address:

_____

Sentence	Purpose	Content
1	Introductory sentence	
2	Explain general features	
3	Focus on one particular feature	
4	Sum up and make clear who it is suitable for	

Star rating (1 to 5) _____

Book review

Title: _____ ISBN: _____

Author: _____ Publisher: _____

Sentence	Purpose	Content
1	Introductory sentence	
2	Explain general content and style	
3	Give details of good or bad points	
4	Sum up and make clear who it is suitable for	

Star rating (1 to 5) _____

- Write your reviews.

NOW TRY THIS!

- Rewrite one of your reviews. This time, write it for teachers who want to find out what things young people like and why.
- Make notes about the changes you make to the language and style.

Teachers' note Stress to the pupils that there are no 'wrong answers' when writing reviews, and that all opinions, if supported with adequate evidence, are acceptable. Encourage them to think carefully about their reactions to the book (or other product) and how they think other readers or users might react.

Take a view
STARTER

- What are your views on vegetarianism? Look at the pictures. Think about the issue of vegetarianism from each different point of view.

Meat-eater

Farm animals

Should you have a right to eat meat if you want to? What might happen if meat production were reduced?

Farmer

Pets

- Make notes for a speech about your views on vegetarianism. Think of how you can use examples and evidence to support your point of view.

My views on vegetarianism	Examples	Evidence

Teachers' note Give each pupil a copy of this page. Allow five minutes for them to consider the arguments for and against vegetarianism and to make notes about their personal point of view. Invite a pupil to state his or her view, giving examples and evidence and using persuasive language. Then ask if anyone can give a contrasting point of view, again supported by evidence. Encourage other pupils to voice objections to any of the arguments expressed, and give the original speakers the chance to defend their opinions. See also the activity on pages 52–53.

Developing Literacy
Text Level
Year 7
© A & C BLACK

Take a view

• Choose one of these statements. Decide whether or not you agree with it.

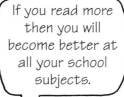

Boxing is a violent and dangerous sport and should be banned.

School on a Saturday should be compulsory for all pupils who fail to complete their work during the week.

If you read more then you will become better at all your school subjects.

Girls' football teams should be given the same opportunities and funding as boys' football teams.

• Plan a speech to present your point of view.

My point of view: _____

_____

Examples to support my argument

(1) _____ (2) _____

_____ _____

_____ _____

Evidence to support my argument

(1) _____ (2) _____

_____ _____

_____ _____

Useful ways of opening sentences

Introducing examples and evidence:

   For instance…
   It is well known that…
   Consider the case of…

Confirming my point of view:

   Therefore…
   Clearly…
   Without doubt…

_____ _____

_____ _____

_____ _____

NOW TRY THIS!

• List points other people might make to argue against your point of view.

• Make notes to help you defend your point of view against these arguments.

Teachers' note Discuss how an argument can be illustrated with examples (individual cases) and evidence (which proves a general trend). When the pupils have completed the activity sheet, allow them the opportunity to give their speeches, then for others to challenge the arguments with opposing points of view, and for the original speakers to defend their opinions.

Developing Literacy
Text Level
Year 7
© A & C BLACK **57**

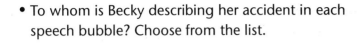

Identify the typical features of spoken texts

The way it's said

STARTER

- To whom is Becky describing her accident in each speech bubble? Choose from the list.

1

It was that Jack's fault. 'E shoved me on the steps. You should've seen my ankle. It was up like a balloon and hurting like mad. I 'ad to go to the 'ozzy to get X-rayed.

A Her baby brother
B Her best friend
C The doctor

3

I fell. It's sore. That's why I've got a bandage, but it'll get better.

2

I slipped down the steps when someone pushed me. It's hurting here… and here. I can't put any weight on my right foot.

- To whom is Becky's mum talking in each speech bubble? Choose from the list.

D A colleague
E Becky
F A customer

4

Good morning, madam. We can arrange to come on Monday. Would 10 o'clock be convenient?

6

Hi Jean, 10 a.m. Monday OK for the work at Tree Tops?

5

Hello, love. I'll pick you up from Shona's at 10. OK?

Teachers' note Photocopy this page onto an OHT. Read speech bubbles 1 to 3 in role and ask the pupils to notice the different tones of voice you use as well as the differences between what you say each time. The pupils could then read speech bubbles 4 to 6 in role. Invite the others to comment on whether they would read the words differently. Identify the audience of the words in each speech bubble and write the letters in the boxes. Draw out the idea that people naturally alter the way in which they speak depending on the audience.

58

Developing Literacy
Text Level
Year 7
© A & C BLACK

The way it's said

- Listen to an informal interview and a more formal one.
- Look out for the features on the chart in formal and informal spoken language. Tick or cross to show whether you find them. Record examples.

It'll be fair claggy and walsh – aye an' the odd thunner pash.

I take it that we shall experience damp, misty weather, scattered showers and the occasional thunderstorm?

Language features	Formal ✔ or ✗	Informal ✔ or ✗	Examples
Slang words			
Dialect expressions			
Contractions			
Jargon			
Exclamations			
Non-standard English formations:			
Double negatives			
Non-agreement of nouns/verbs			
Non-agreement of pronouns/verbs			
Non-standard verb formations			
Other			

NOW TRY THIS!

- With a partner, plan a short interview of a pop singer for a radio show for young listeners.
- Enact the interview.
- How could you adapt it into an interview of an opera singer for a classical music programme? Make notes on the changes you would make.

Teachers' note Before the lesson, record suitable radio or television interviews – one fairly formal and the other informal. Introduce or revise the language features on the chart (see page 64). Then play the recordings and ask the pupils to note down which of the features are present. During the plenary session, discuss the differences between the type of language used in each interview.

Save me!

STARTER

This hot-air balloon is losing power. Only one passenger can remain in the basket, otherwise the balloon will crash-land.

• Which passenger would you choose to save? Why?

Why would you not save the others?

Senior citizen

Shop assistant

Student

Farmer

Doctor

Teachers' note Split the class into groups of four or five, and give each group a copy of this page. Ask the groups to decide which passenger they would save, and let them work out for themselves how they will do this. If, as is likely, the members of the group begin with different choices, they must justify their own choice and try to convince the others. In order to make a final decision, they may have to vote. After five to ten minutes, invite feedback from the groups and ask them how they agreed on their choice.

Developing Literacy
Text Level
Year 7
© A & C BLACK

Save me!

- Choose a person to represent in a | balloon debate |.
- Only one passenger in the balloon can be saved.
  Plan a speech to persuade an audience to choose you.
  Make notes on the clipboard.

> Research the person you are representing. Use the language and expressions he or she would use.

!

Name of person I am representing:

Notes for speech	Research notes
Grab the audience's attention	
Important achievements	
Useful skills and knowledge	
Conclusion	

You could start humorously or with a dramatic opening sentence.

Appeal to the audience with details of things you have done.

Make the audience think about how it will affect others if you are not saved.

Sum up. Emphasise the important points.

NOW TRY THIS!

- The audience (and other characters in the debate) will challenge some of the things you say. Think about the points they might challenge and prepare replies.
- Plan questions to ask the other characters in the debate.

  Example: *In what ways do you improve the lives of other people?*

Teachers' note Explain to the pupils that they may choose any character to represent, from fiction or a real person (living or from history). Encourage them to research their chosen character thoroughly and to plan the speech 'in role'. When the speeches are prepared, conduct a balloon debate using four or five of the characters and let the audience decide which should be saved.

Developing Literacy
Text Level
Year 7
© A & C BLACK **61**

Speech detectives
STARTER

- Read the passage.
- What does it tell you about the characters and the relationship between them? Make notes on the chart.

Look at the vocabulary, **tone**, sentence structures and level of formality.

'How's the bellyache, then?'

Gwyn stuck his head round the door.

'A bore,' said Alison. 'And I'm too hot.'

'Tough,' said Gwyn, 'I couldn't find any books, so I've brought one I had from school. I'm supposed to be reading it for English, but you're welcome: it looks deadly.'

'Thanks anyway,' said Alison.

'Roger's gone for a swim. You wanting company, are you?'

'Don't put yourself out for me,' said Alison.

'Right,' said Gwyn. 'Cheerio.'

He rode sideways down the banisters.

'Gwyn!'

'Yes? What's the matter? You OK?'

'Quick!'

'You want a basin? You going to throw up, are you?'

'Gwyn!'

He ran back. Alison was kneeling on the bed.

'Listen,' she said. 'Can you hear that?'

'That what?'

'That noise in the ceiling. Listen.'

From *The Owl Service* by Alan Garner

	Alison	Evidence	Gwyn	Evidence
Age				
Personality				
Relationship to other character				

Teachers' note Photocopy this page onto an OHT. Invite two pupils to read the passage in role and ask the others to deduce from the spoken words how old the characters are, what their personalities are like, and what the relationship between them might be. Ensure that the pupils back up all their deductions with evidence. Explain that the tone of spoken words is the way in which they are said. Discuss how the use of slang, non-standard sentence grammar, contractions and exclamations contribute to the informal style of the dialogue.

62

Developing Literacy
Text Level
Year 7
© A & C BLACK

Speech detectives

- Imagine that Gwyn is an elderly, well-to-do gentleman. How do you think the vocabulary, **tone** and sentence structure of the spoken words would change? Rewrite the passage.

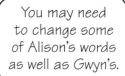

You may need to change some of Alison's words as well as Gwyn's.

'Gwyn!'

'Yes? What's the matter? You OK?'

'Quick!'

'You want a basin? You going to throw up, are you?'

'Gwyn!'

He ran back. Alison was kneeling on the bed.

'Listen,' she said. 'Can you hear that?'

'That what?'

'That noise in the ceiling. Listen.'

The house was quiet… and something was scratching in the ceiling above the bed.

'Mice,' said Gwyn.

'Too loud,' said Alison.

'Rats, then.'

'No. Listen. It's something hard.'

'They want their claws trimming.'

From *The Owl Service* by Alan Garner

NOW TRY THIS!

- Compare your rewritten dialogue with the original passage.
- Make notes on the kinds of changes you made, and why.

Teachers' note First discuss how to alter the dialogue to show the change in relationship between the two speakers. The sentences will be longer and more formal, and it is likely that Alison would address the other speaker as Mr… (the pupils could make up a name). You could ask two pupils to act out a new version of the dialogue in role before the others write their own versions.

Glossary

accent The way in which words are pronounced, including: how 'open' or 'closed' vowel sounds are; the level of hardness of consonants; the emphasis or dropping of initial and final consonants; and the stress on syllables.

active (of a verb) A verb whose subject does the action: for example, *they shouted.*

adjective A word that describes a noun: for example, *blue, round, tall.*

adverb A word that gives information about a verb: for example, *she shouted loudly.*

agreement The match between words or phrases in terms of number, gender, case and person: for example, a singular noun requires a singular verb (*she goes, he walks*).

alliteration The repetition of a letter or sound at the beginning of words: for example, *lizards lounging lazily.*

balloon debate A debate in which the speakers take on roles and try to convince an audience that they should be saved from a hot-air balloon which is losing power.

chronological writing Writing organised so that events follow a time sequence.

connective A word or phrase used to link words, phrases, clauses, sentences or paragraphs: for example, *I like swimming but Jane prefers running; we go there whenever we can.*

contraction A shortened form of a word in which an apostrophe replaces omitted letters: for example, *you're (you are).*

dialect A form of slang used in a place. It includes non-standard English words such as *gan* for 'go' (northeast England) and *bairn* for 'child' (Scotland and northeast England). Dialect varies from town to town and region to region.

double negative The use of two negatives where only one is needed: for example, *I didn't say nothing.*

ellipsis (plural *ellipses*) Three dots (...) which show that words in a passage have been missed out. Ellipses are also used to show that spoken words or a train of thought are trailing off.

fact A statement which can be checked and verified in more than one source.

fiction An invented version of events – the creation of the writer.

genre A term used to describe different kinds of writing, each characterised by particular features: for example, science fiction, mystery.

imperative The command form of a verb: for example, *go, mix, take.*

jargon A form of language which includes technical terms and is used by members of a group: for example, politicians, sailors or chess-players.

key words and phrases The important words and phrases in a passage, which indicate its topic.

metaphor A comparison which says one thing *is* the other: for example, *the river is a ribbon of moonlight.*

mood (of a text) The emotional 'feel'.

non-chronological writing Writing that does not follow the restrictions of a time sequence: for example, a report organised according to characteristics.

non-standard English Spoken or written language which includes the use of unconventional grammar. It may contain slang and dialect expressions.

noun A word that names a person, place or thing: for example, *a river, the Thames, a tributary.*

onomatopoeia The use of words which make sounds associated with their meanings: for example, *boom, squeak.*

passive (of a verb) A verb whose subject has the action done to it: for example, *the ball was kicked by the girl; the money was stolen.*

person (of a verb) This can be singular or plural: for example, *I go, we go* (first person); *you go* (second person); *she goes, they go* (third person).

pronoun A word used instead of a noun: for example, *he, them, it.*

rhetorical question A question asked for persuasive effect, which does not require an answer from the audience.

scan To look at a text quickly, to locate key words and ideas.

simile A comparison which uses *like* or *as*: for example, *she sang like an angel.*

skim To read a passage to gain an overview of the subject matter.

slang A form of non-standard English which is used by different groups of people, according to where they live and their interests (unlike dialect, slang is not confined to an area, although dialects include slang expressions).

standard English Spoken or written language which uses the conventional rules of grammar.

syllable A rhythmic sound unit of a word. Each syllable should contain at least one vowel or a *y*: for example, *al/though* has two syllables; *syl/lab/le* has three.

synonyms Words with the same or similar meanings: for example, *joy, happiness, delight.*

tense The form of a verb that indicates time (past, present or future).

tone The way in which something is expressed: for example, ironically or casually. In writing, language and punctuation help to convey tone.

verb A word or group of words that indicates action or a state of being: for example, *is, grew.*

Developing Literacy: Text Level Year 7 © A & C BLACK